W9-BZO-952

WOMEN

AT PLAY

WOMEN AT PLAY

The Story of Women in Baseball

Barbara Gregorich

A Harvest Original

Harcourt

Brace &

Company

SAN DIEGO   NEW YORK   LONDON

For Robin, Rory, and Bonnie
and to the memory of Maud Nelson

Copyright © 1993 by Barbara Gregorich

All rights reserved. No part of this publication may be reproduced or transmitted in any form or by any means, electronic or mechanical, including photocopy, recording, or any information storage and retrieval system, without permission in writing from the publisher.

Requests for permission to make copies of any part of the work should be mailed to: Permissions Department, Harcourt Brace & Company, 8th Floor, Orlando, Florida 32887.

Library of Congress Cataloging-in-Publication Data
Gregorich, Barbara.
Women at play: the story of women in baseball/Barbara Gregorich.—1st ed.
p.   cm.
"A Harvest original."
Includes index.
ISBN 0-15-698297-8
1. Women baseball players—United States. 2. Women baseball players—United States—Biography. 3. All-American Girls Professional Baseball League—History. 4. Baseball—United States—History—20th century. I. Title.
GV880.7.G74   1993
796.357′64′ 0973—dc20   93-16223

Designed by Trina Stahl
Printed in the United States of America
First edition
A B C D E
Photo and permissions acknowledgments appear on page 209, which constitutes a continuation of the copyright page.

Contents

Introduction

BASEBALL: FOR A SIMPLE GAME, IT'S ENTICINGLY COMPLEX.
Filled with banter, it is home to the deep silence of tragedy. The
game that includes so much has also included women.

Girls and women have played baseball (hardball: the real
thing) from the beginning. Not long after professional baseball
began in 1869, women formed "base ball clubs" and, wearing
heavy stockings and striped, shortened dresses, took to diamonds
across the nation. Organized into barnstorming Bloomer Girl
teams, they challenged men's teams to town, semipro, and minor-
league baseball games everywhere. In those early days, the
sixteen-year-old pitching phenom, Maud Nelson, started her long
baseball career. Among the middle class, baseball between the
sexes was considered so improper that male university students
who dared to accept the Bloomer challenge were sometimes ex-
pelled. But the common people applauded women. Pitcher Lizzie
Arlington was given a minor-league contract, and umpire Amanda
Clement received top billing and top dollar.

With the end of World War I, both baseball and women became
bolder. Bloomer teams proliferated under nonbloomer names: the
Philadelphia Bobbies, Chicago All-Star Athletic Girls, American

yes

Athletic Girls, and All-Star Ranger Girls. In small towns, young girls like Margaret Gisolo helped lead baseball teams to state championships through perfect fielding and clutch hitting. Jackie Mitchell and Babe Didrikson struck out major-leaguers during spring exhibition games, with fans, reporters, and movie crews as witness.

In 1943 the first and (thus far) only women's professional baseball league was born, the All-American Girls Baseball League. Approximately six hundred women, all of them skilled in a wide variety of sports—from the high jump to handball to skating and basketball and bowling—earned a living by playing on all-women's baseball teams against other such teams. The AAGBL gave its players advantages no other female ballplayers had before or since—the money of Philip K. Wrigley and the dedication and skill of former major-leaguers, who taught them how to perfect their baseball skills.

The years between the demise of the All-American Girls Baseball League in 1954 and the rise of integrated Little League in 1974 constituted a period of doldrums for women. Toni Stone spent one year in the Negro League majors and played fifty games—but was still better off than Eleanor Engle, who was signed by the minor-league Harrisburg Senators and then banished from the game forever.

With the integration of Little League, female ballplayers such as Amy Dickinson in the 1970s and Angela Zampella and Brianne Stepherson in the 1990s showed the world how well girls can play baseball and inspired women to try to integrate the organized game. With a mostly female roster, the Sun Sox of 1984, sponsored by former Atlanta Braves public relations director Bob Hope, tried to win the minor-league franchise for Daytona Beach, Florida. In the world of umpires, the men in blue were suddenly working with women in blue: Bernice Gera, Christine Wren, and Pam Postema all umpired in the minor leagues. And on the college level, women such as Robyn Stockton, Kim Douthett, and Julie Croteau took their turn playing baseball.

Thousands of women have played baseball. Their names are on the crumbling pages of forgotten newspapers, their stories waiting to be told. The telling will serve as the first step in breaking baseball's last and most formidable barrier—the one that has kept women from their rightful place in the professional game.

Acknowledgments

HUNDREDS OF PEOPLE HAVE HELPED ME COLLECT INFORMATION for the hidden history of women in baseball, generously mailing me newspaper clippings, suggesting sources, granting me interviews, and lending me photographs. I thank all of them wholeheartedly.

My special thanks to the following: who have helped beyond measure: Dr. Robert K. Adair; Don Allan; Isabel Alvarez; Al Barloga; Peter C. Bjarkman; Wilma Briggs; Helen Clement; Jack Clement; Dottie Wiltse Collins; Kit Crissey; Julie Croteau; Millie Deegan; Joe and Evelyn Dellacqua; Jean Faut Eastman; Madeline English; Jay Feldman; Bill Friday; Rose Gacioch; Larry Gerlach; Margaret Gisolo; Kevin Grace; Ray Hisrich; Bill Hockenbury;

Mary Gilroy Hockenbury; John Holway; Edith Houghton; Roy
Hughes; Allen Hye; David Jenkins; Steve Johnson; Dottie
Kamenshek; Colin Kapitan; Robin Koontz; Sophie Kurys; Larry
Lester; James Mote; Yoichi Nagata; Bill Plott; Louise Clement
Ragsdale; Dick Reynolds; Mark Rucker; Florence Bouffard
Sagan; Helen Callaghan St. Aubin; Dottie Schroeder; Fred
Schuld; Ouisie Shapiro; Mike Sparrow; Joanne Winter; Connie
Wisniewski; Dr. Lois Youngen.

My special thanks as well to these organizations and insti-
tutions: Amateur Athletic Foundation, Wayne Wilson; *Atlanta
Journal-Constitution*, Kay Pinckney and Pam Prouty; Indiana State
Library; Manchester Historic Association, Elizabeth Lessard;
Minnesota Historical Society, Patricia Harpole; National Baseball
Hall of Fame and Museum, Bill Deane and Robert Browning;
Northern Indiana Historical Society, Diane Barts and Carol
Pickerl; Oak Park Public Library; Public Museum of Grand Rapids,
Marilyn Merdzinski; Rockford Public Library; SABR, the Society
for American Baseball Research; Watervliet Public Library,
Cindy Young; Women's Sports Foundation.

Finally, my thanks to Sharon Sliter Johnson, who volunteered to
serve as my research assistant and helped me track the footsteps
of Maud Nelson; to Rory Metcalf, who searched Staten Island for
the legacy of Margaret Nabel and the New York Bloomer Girls; to
Jane Jordan Browne, my agent, who offered invaluable critiques
of the manuscript; to John Radziewicz, my editor, who believed in
the book and suggested its structure; and to Phil Passen, my husband and best baseball companion, for all of the above and more.

Part 1

THE
EARLY
YEARS

IN THE MID-NINETEENTH CENTURY, THE BALL-AND-STICK games that Americans had played for a century evolved into the game of baseball. A few years after its rules were formalized by the New York Knickerbocker Club in 1845, baseball was being played by teams of "nines," "eights," or "sevens" on green fields and empty lots throughout New York City. Soon the nation, too, caught baseball fever.

The game quickly turned professional when the Cincinnati Red Stockings fielded a team of paid players in 1869. In short order, professional baseball teams were formed in most eastern cities. The game was in its infancy—recognizable as the game we now play, but less regulated and marked by features that seem most unusual today. Batters were out if the fielder caught the ball on the first bounce, and fielders wore no gloves until the 1870s. Pitchers threw underhand until 1883 and from a distance of fifty feet until 1893, and catchers, standing well behind the plate, caught the pitch on a bounce. While three strikes constituted an out, the number of balls it took to draw a walk varied between five and nine until 1889. Home runs were rare, seven a year considered magnificent.

The ball itself varied only slightly from today's, perhaps a half-inch greater in circumference and a half-ounce heavier. Bats, on the other hand, weighed forty-eight ounces or more and had handles almost as wide as the thick end of the bat. Today's bats are svelte, with thinner handles, a more tapered shape, and an average weight of thirty-three ounces.

Back then, players such as Albert G. Spalding, a pitcher who went on to start a sporting-goods business and write baseball guides, considered baseball "too strenuous for womankind." In nineteenth-century America, women did not have the right to vote; could not own property after marriage; could not divorce; and could not receive an education. They were not permitted to dress in functional clothing or engage in competitive games. An axiom of the times was that a woman's name should appear in print but twice in a lifetime: when she married and when she died. Certainly not when she graduated from college—and positively not when she drove in a game-winning run.

In their struggle for equal rights, women turned to female colleges. Vassar was founded in 1865, both Smith and Wellesley in 1875. There, free to play, women took up baseball. Wasting no time, Vassar students formed two baseball clubs in 1866. Ten years later, the Vassar Resolutes even had uniforms of sorts: long-sleeved shirts with frilled high necklines, belts embroidered with the team name, RESOLUTES, wide floor-length skirts, high-button shoes, and broadly striped caps that look much like the Montreal Expos' headgear of the 1970s and 1980s.

Restricted to layers of cumbersome clothing that weighed up to thirty pounds, a college student playing baseball at Smith in the 1870s had to hit the ball, drop the bat, lift the train of her long skirt, drape it over her arm, and—if she wasn't already out—dash to first. Even after Amelia Bloomer, one of the early pioneers of women's rights, designed and wore the loose-fitting Turkish trousers that came to be called bloomers, the style met with such controversy that few women adopted it. The promise of bloomers lived on, however, and when women began to play serious professional baseball in the 1890s, their teams were called Bloomer Girls for the clothing they wore.

In the women's colleges, teams played baseball every weekend. But in coeducational institutions, women were forbidden to play the game. At the University of Pennsylvania in 1904, five female students joined a men's baseball game. According to a newspaper, "the news spread and in a short time there was a crowd of cheering students. Each play or misplay in which the gentle sex had a part, was applauded long and loud and pandemonium finally broke loose when one of the stalwart 'co-eds' knocked out a two-bagger. But the attention of the faculty had been attracted and the result was the prohibition." University authorities ruled that women who wanted to play baseball "must not do so on the college campus," and the bursar notified the police to stop all such games.

Outside the colleges, several male promoters came up with the idea of forming women's baseball teams and charging the public admission to see them play. The first women to play baseball for pay took the field in Springfield, Illinois, in 1875. Nobody, however, considered them professional ballplayers. The Blondes and Brunettes who competed in that first game weren't athletes but adventurous spirits who entertained the spectators with bad baseball and laughable scores (42–38 in six innings). Traveling to cities such as Philadelphia, New York, and New Orleans, the Blondes and Brunettes (or the Reds and Blues, as they were sometimes named) played miserable baseball until the mid-1880s, when they disappeared from the scene. The public had tired of farce.

But the determined students and the droll entertainers were the precursors of the first *professional* female baseball players, the Bloomer Girls of the 1890s. On bloomer teams, women played the game, played it well, and received good pay for doing so. One generation after the Red Stockings went professional, female baseball players—Albert G. Spalding's pronouncements notwithstanding—were hitting one- and two-baggers, stealing bases, and knocking out home runs.

Of the hundreds of bloomer teams that played between 1890 and 1920, a few were composed of rowdies whose main interest was carousing. These soon faded, while the serious teams—the Boston Bloomer Girls, the Star Bloomers, and the Western Bloomer Girls—lasted for decades because they offered the public exciting baseball. Naturals such as Maud Nelson shaped history: for forty years Nelson pitched, played third base, scouted, and owned or managed bloomer teams. Other baseball pioneers made their own openings. Amanda Clement became a highly respected umpire in the semipro leagues throughout the Dakotas; Alta Weiss pitched throughout Ohio and Kentucky, even taking the mound in Cleveland's major league stadium, League Park.

The early years tell a story of baseball heroes—pioneers who couldn't be brushed back, who dug in and played the game. When baseball touched these women, it transformed their lives.

Maud Nelson

"The Boston Bloomers, ladies' champion baseball club of the world, will cross bats with the All-Portlands this afternoon at Portland field. These clever ladies put up an interesting and scientific game, full of fun and funny features. Judging from the many flattering notices they have received, the All-Portland nine will have to 'play ball' to win. It is worth the price of admission alone to see Miss Nelson, the phenomenal pitcher. She has speed and curves. Game called at 3 o'clock."

—*The Oregonian*, October 3, 1897

SOME PLAY BASEBALL FOR A DAY AND CALL IT QUITS, finding the complexities of spin, swing, and hop too baffling to master. Some play it for decades and grow into legends: Cobb and Johnson, Aaron and Mays, Fisk and Ryan. Maud Nelson is one of the latter, a legend who dominated the early years of women at play. She was a world-renowned Bloomer Girl pitcher, a third baseman, a scout, a manager, and an owner of the best teams of her era. She played for the Boston Bloomers and the Star Bloomers, created the Western Bloomer Girls, the American Athletic Girls, and the All Star Ranger Girls. For forty years she was always there.

Yet almost nobody today has heard of Maud Nelson. The few books in which she's mentioned cite her only as a bloomer pitcher at the turn of the century. Certainly one reason for her obscurity is the general neglect of historians toward women in baseball. Another was Maud's natural modesty. She was a person who lived for the excitement of the moment. Mary Gilroy, who played for Maud in 1922 in New Orleans, never knew that her manager had been the most famous pitcher of the early bloomer days. Margaret Gisolo toured with the All Star Ranger Girls *for five years* in the 1930s and had no idea that Maud had been a player. Another reason for Maud's obscurity is that in her lifetime she traveled under many different names—Brida, Nelson, Nielson, Olson, and Dellacqua.

Although little is known about her childhood, from the time this dark-haired, dark-eyed pitcher stepped on the mound at the age of sixteen, her life was baseball. Approximately five feet, three inches tall, with a serious demeanor and a formidable pitching arsenal, Maud took the small towns from Maine to Oregon and Michigan to Florida by storm. In 1897, Maud Nelson (sometimes reported as Maude Nielson) was the starting pitcher for the barnstorming Boston Bloomer Girls, who by October of that year had traveled all the way to Oregon, where the *Eugene Guard* reported that "the girls from Beantown put up a clean game and play like professionals, asking for no favors, but playing a hard snappy game on its merits."

Born November 17, 1881, in a Tyrolean village, Clementina Brida was very young when her family emigrated to the United States. It's not known where she grew up, who taught her to pitch, or how she got the name Maud Nelson, but her traces suggest some industrialized northern city such as Boston, Pittsburgh, or Chicago. Just as playing baseball helped Americanize young immigrant boys (a theme common in baseball literature), the national game helped Americanize this young Italian girl.

As a pitcher she won praise everywhere. In 1900, when her bloomer team played Union City, Indiana, the *Cincinnati Enquirer* reported: "The bloomer girls defeated the Union City team [3–1] here to-day in a well-played game. The feature was the pitching of the Misses Maude Nelson and Edith Lindsay, only

Maud Nelson in her early pitching days

three hits being made off them." Young Brida pitched so well that it was a bad day when she gave up four hits. Often she struck out the side for the first two or three innings, then turned the game over to another pitcher: Maud, the star attraction and main draw, had to pitch every day.

Her longevity further confirms her talent. In 1908, at age twenty-seven, she started for the Cherokee Indian Base Ball Club as it toured Michigan and Canada. At thirty-three she was still going strong for the American Athletic Girls. And in 1922,

Postcard of the Cherokee Indian team:

John Olson, seated, far left

OLSON'S CHEROKEE INDIAN BASE BALL TEAM, WATERVLIET, MICH

at forty-one, she made guest pitching appearances for the Boston Bloomer Girls.

Other women who gained fame as pitchers—Alta Weiss and Jackie Mitchell among them—would play first base or the outfield when their innings were over. Not Maud. In late innings she played third base—the hot corner, where players must stop bullets, recover, and make the long throw to first base with great accuracy and velocity. That Nelson played this position, particularly in late innings, testifies to her skills and instincts. And whatever her position in the field, her bat could be relied upon to produce hits.

At thirty, Nelson became owner-manager of the Western Bloomer Girls in 1911 with her first husband, John B. Olson, Jr. From that year on she also served as a scout of both male and female players, recruiting the most promising to one or another of her many teams.

Her players remember her as quiet and modest. Her most widely distributed picture, in which she's wearing a round cap and gripping a baseball, reveals her utterly serious side. But a picture of her sitting cross-legged among the Western Bloomer Girls shows a woman happy and at ease. Maud got things done: trained the players, consulted the booking agents, and handled the daily emergencies of injured, homesick, or has-been players. Quality was what she strove for. She once wrote to Toney Gisolo, whose sister Margaret she was considering for the All Star Ranger Girls, that in order to play on her team, both brother and sister had to be good. "No fake attractions," she warned.

After her husband died in 1917, Maud toured with the Boston

"Mr. Olson has added a special attraction to his great Indian Club in the person of Maude Nelson, Champion Lady Base Ball Pitcher of the world. The lady pitcher has enjoyed the distinction of being the greatest all-around female ball player in existence. She inaugurated the season of 1908 for the Cherokee Indian Club at Hartford, Michigan, on May 15, by pitching the first two innings of the game and made the remarkable record of retiring the side twice with eleven pitched balls."

—The Watervliet Record,
May 22, 1908

Bloomer Girls again. She also managed a women's team for the Chicago Athletic Club, barnstorming the South and playing exhibition games on Pelican Field in New Orleans.

In 1922 or 1923 (reports vary), she met and married Costante Dellacqua, a widower from Italy who worked as a chef in a Chicago hotel. Maud raised young Joe Dellacqua, her stepson, who recalls that one day she said to his father: "Let's start a baseball team." And thus the All Star Ranger Girls were born.

If it hadn't been for Maud Nelson, three generations of women would have missed the chance to play professional baseball. Countless women who played the national pastime from 1897 through 1935 played with or for Maud, or on one of the many

The Star Bloomer Girls: Maud Nelson in back row, far right

teams that she started and then sold: Lizzie Arlington, Carrie Nation, Kate Becker, Ruth Woods, Jane James, Alice Lopes, Tex Wines, Elizabeth Pull, Beatrice Schmidt, Margaret Gisolo, Rose Gacioch.

When the Depression made it more and more difficult to field a baseball team, when women began playing softball rather than baseball, and when her oldest players retired and her youngest went off to other jobs, Maud Nelson Olson Dellacqua retired with Costante to a house one long throw from Wrigley Field. There she died February 15, 1944. She was the first and the greatest: the reliable starter and the keeper of the flame.

BLOOMER GIRLS

During the 1890s, scores of women's baseball teams sprang up across the country, calling themselves Bloomer Girls after the clothing they wore. One of the first such teams originated in Wapakoneta, Ohio, where a Mr. A. P. Gibbs managed various bloomer teams from 1892 through at least 1912, possibly well into the 1920s.

Belonging to no league, all bloomer teams were barnstormers, traveling to nearby states or across the country, challenging men's town, semipro, and minor league teams to games. Although bloomers seldom played one another, there are instances, particularly during the 1920s and 1930s, in which they did compete, as when the New York Bloomer Girls played against the Philadelphia Bobbies, or the Bobbies played the Chicago Bloomers.

They were called Bloomer *Girl* teams not because they were composed entirely of women, but because the majority of the players were female—much as a men's team is called men's even when (as in the case of Jackie Mitchell and the Junior Lookouts or Babe Didrikson and the House of David) there is a woman or two on it. The earliest of these sexually integrated teams carried at least one male player: the catcher. Later teams carried two, three, and occasionally four male players: usually the additional men played short, third, or center field. Hall-of-Famers Smokey Joe Wood and Rogers Hornsby played on bloomer girl teams in their youth.

In the earliest days, male bloomer players were called toppers and occasionally wore wigs and skirts in order to pass as women. But after ballplaying women discarded their skirts and bloomers and stepped into traditional baseball pants, males stopped posing as females—although as late as the 1930s, ballpark announcers and sports reporters thought it

humorous to call a male player by a female name. Thus a Charles Smith would be announced as "Miss Charlotte Smith, catcher."

Fired by competitive drive and thrilled to play baseball, the bloomers endured the hardships and earned the victories. The Boston Bloomer Girls of 1903 once played and won twenty-eight games in twenty-six days. In the small town of Sapulpa, Oklahoma, they recorded an 8–1 win on July 3, took a July 4 doubleheader from a Tulsa team (11–0 and 11–3), and shut out the teams in Skiatook, Owasso, and Ochalata.

In their more traditional baseball clothing, using names such as the American Athletic Girls or the All Star Ranger Girls, these sexually integrated barnstorming teams lasted until the mid-1930s.

Lizzie Arlington

As THE FIRST WOMAN SIGNED TO A CONTRACT IN THE minor leagues, Lizzie Arlington holds a unique place in baseball history. Still, surprisingly little is known about her. This much is certain: she was signed for two reasons but let go for one—signed because she was a woman and a good ballplayer, let go only because she was a woman.

The young Elizabeth Stride grew up in the coal-mining hills of Mahanoy City, Pennsylvania—the same anthracite country that forged pitcher John Elmer Stivetts, who entered the majors in 1889 with St. Louis, then jumped to Boston, where in 1892 he won thirty-five games for the world champions. Although Lizzie Stride (remembered as Lizzie Stroud in reports fifty years later) grew up playing baseball with her father and brothers, it was Jack Stivetts who helped her perfect her pitching.

Seeing the short but sturdy young woman pitch, a promoter named William J. Conner became her manager, paying her $100 a week to start for professional teams. On July 2, 1898, the twenty-two-year-old, who used the name Lizzie Arlington when playing ball, appeared in her first professional game, pitching four in-nings for the Philadelphia Reserves and giving up six hits and

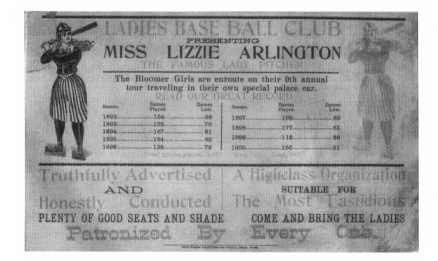

Lizzie Arlington as promoted by A. P. Gibbs

"Miss Arlington with several other persons drove on the grounds in a stylish carriage drawn by two white horses. To the applause that greeted her she lifted her cap. The spectators beheld a plump young woman with attractive face and rosy cheeks. She wore a gray uniform with skirt coming to the knees, black stockings and a jaunty cap. Her hair was not cropped short, but was done up in the latest fashion.

"She practiced with Reading and played 2nd base. She made several stops, but the very hot 'daisy-cutters' she left to Ulrich. She made several neat throws. She went about it like a professional, even down to expectorating on her hands and wiping her hands on her uniform. Miss Arlington was put in in the 9th when Reading was 5 tallies to the good. Joe Delahanty, the first batter to face her, fouled to Heydon. Lyons shoved a little grounder to the female twirler, who threw him out at 1st. Seagrave and Jim Delahanty made safe cracks and Boyle walked. With the bases full, Cleve gave Newell a foul. 'Good for Lizzie,' shrieked the crowd. She shook hands with a number. Miss Arlington might do as a pitcher among amateurs, but the sluggers of the Atlantic League would soon put her out of the business. She, of course, hasn't the strength to get much speed on and has poor control. But, for a woman, she is a success. . . ."

—*The Reading Eagle*, July 5, 1898

three unearned runs. At the plate, she collected two hits off former big leaguer Mike Kilroy and finished the game at second base as the Reserves defeated Richmond, 18–5.

Calculating that the crowds would turn out in large numbers to see a woman pitch, Conner had hoped to make a lot of money with his new property. He was sorely disappointed. Despite the big promotion, only five hundred turned out to witness the game. Still, the novelty of using a woman pitcher appealed to another baseball man of the time, young Edward Grant Barrow, president of the Atlantic League and later chief executive of the New York Yankees during the Ruth-Gehrig era. Sufficiently intrigued, Barrow signed Arlington. On July 5, 1898, she pitched in a regulation minor league game for Reading against Allentown, appearing in the ninth inning, when Reading was ahead 5–0, and giving up no runs. Approximately one thousand people (including two hundred women) turned out to see the game.

Barrow, like Conner, believed that the novelty of a female pitcher would attract more gate money. When that failed to happen, Arlington and her high salary were let go. Had she been a male player with the same abilities, there would have been a spot for her in the minors at a lesser salary—but nobody in the world of organized men's baseball could conceive of a woman as simply another player on the team.

Although her career in the minors was brief, Lizzie Arlington signed up with a bloomer team and continued to play baseball for years. In 1900 she was pitching for A. P. Gibbs's team out of Wapakoneta, Ohio. Ironically, she was signed to play for the Bloomer Girls for the very same reasons she was signed to play in the

"The sensible thing, I would think, is to accept or reject a player on merit alone. I admit that I signed Lizzie strictly as a stunt. But I'm not so sure she couldn't win a spot somewhere in organized ball if she were in her prime today."
—Edward Grant Barrow, on minor league commissioner George Trautman barring women baseball players in 1952

minors—because she was a woman and because she was a good player. But playing on a team composed mainly of women, she wasn't an individual novelty; and if the relationship between the salaries of stars and nonstars on later bloomer teams is any indication, she probably received pay equal to or only marginally higher than that of the other players. If somewhere down the line an owner failed to sign Arlington to a bloomer team, it was only because of her playing ability, not because of her sex.

Amanda Clement

IN THE SETTLING OF THE WEST, MANY PIONEER WOMEN worked alongside the men, helping to push wagons and clear fields. Harriet Clement was such a woman, one of the first settlers of the southeastern Dakota Territory. Her daughter Amanda, born March 20, 1888, was another pioneer: the first woman paid to umpire a baseball game.

Amanda and her older brother, Hank, grew up in the town of Hudson, South Dakota. Their father died when they were young, and their widowed mother served meals to make money: when the railroad came through, she managed to cook for and feed fifty to seventy-five workers at a time. Amanda, like her mother, could manage large crowds with sole authority and total imperturbability.

Across the street from the Clement house stood Hudson Park, a baseball field where Amanda played with her brother and cousin. When she didn't play, she umpired.

At age sixteen, strictly by accident, she became a professional umpire. The Clements had journeyed to Hawarden, Iowa, where Hank, a semipro pitcher, was to play for the town of Renville. When the umpire scheduled to work the first game (played by amateurs) didn't show up, Hank suggested that his sister take

Eugene F. Clement gave his aunt's hand-carved ivory ball-strike indicator to the Baseball Hall of Fame. He also gave them a smudged baseball dated 1908, with POOR GALLAGHER penned on it. "I'd love to know what happened to poor Gallagher," said Clement, "because I'll bet she threw the son-of-a-buck out of the ball game."

charge. Impressed by her handling of the amateur game, the semipro teams asked the young woman to officiate *their* game—for pay. The Renville-Hawarden game of 1904 thus entered history as the first baseball game umpired by a woman for pay.

Compared to those who came first, today's umpires have it easy: training schools to explain the rules and fellow umpires on the field to serve as buffers against agitated players. At the turn of the century, Amanda Clement stood behind the pitcher's mound, her long hair tucked under her cap, her white shirt crisp, extra baseballs secured in the waistband of her ankle-length blue skirt. "Play ball!" she commanded—and then leaned forward behind the pitcher, the better to call balls and strikes as they sailed

Amanda Clement, umpire

across the plate sixty feet away. As the sole official, she also called all plays at the bases and in the outfield.

Buffeted by the wind, soaked by the rain, and scorched by the sun, she worked semipro games for six years. Between 1904 and 1908, she umpired approximately fifty baseball games a summer, earning from $15 to $25 a game—and receiving top billing for doing so. Whenever there was an important game in the five-state area of the Dakotas, Iowa, Nebraska, and Minnesota, she was the first umpire considered.

Her pay from umpiring put Clement through college: first Yankton Academy in Yankton, South Dakota; then Yankton College. Physically strong and six feet tall, she was an all-round athlete, excelling in basketball, tennis, shot-putting, running sprints, and jumping hurdles. Stories, unofficial and undocumented, say that when she was twenty-four years old she threw a baseball 279 feet (some say 274 or 275 feet, others 294)—a world record for a woman at that time.

Both as a student and an umpire, Amanda Clement was liked and respected. As "the lady in blue," her fame was so widespread that newspapers as far away as Denver and Cincinnati reported on her. One journalist of the time described her as "death on balls and strikes." Death on tantrums, too. She never hesitated to eject a player, once chasing six in a single game.

From Yankton College she went to the University of Nebraska, still umpiring during the baseball season. Later she taught physical education in South Dakota, in North Dakota, and at the University of Wyoming, and later still she managed YMCAs in LaCrosse, Wisconsin, and Keokuk, Iowa. Her varied career

Don Allan, who went on to become the Dean of Students at Yankton College, was eleven years old when Amanda Clement began to board with his widowed mother in Sioux Falls.

"Amanda was a tall, stately lady. She didn't have an ounce of fat on her body and was well-muscled. She looked and walked like a very athletic woman. . . .

"I traveled to Hudson, South Dakota, many times, and I remember seeing her umpire a town team game because the scheduled umpires had not arrived. She went home and put on her long, black skirt and blouse—worked from behind the mound—and there wasn't a peep from anyone on any of her calls. I remember how much in charge she was, and how she conducted herself with so much dignity."

—Letter of December 21, 1989

Clement before retirement as social worker

included work as a justice of the peace, police matron, and type-setter. In 1929, after approximately twenty years of coaching various basketball, tennis, and track teams, Amanda returned to South Dakota to care for her ill mother.

Hank Clement, who continued as a semipro pitcher, married and had six children. Their aunt played baseball with them all, and when she was in her forties she still threw so hard that her nephews put sponges in their gloves to keep their hands from stinging. Neither Amanda's family nor the people of Hudson questioned that she was an umpire. "I took it as a natural thing," says her nephew Jack.

After her mother died in 1934, Amanda moved to Sioux Falls, where she was a social worker for a quarter of a century. In 1964 she was inducted into the South Dakota Sports Hall of Fame, the first umpire chosen. This sturdy pioneer didn't retire until July 1, 1966, at the age of seventy-eight.

On July 20, 1971, Amanda Clement died at the age of eighty-three. Of all her varied accomplishments, it was umpiring she recalled with the most pride. One game in particular epitomized baseball for her, a seventeen-inning contest played in a 100-degree sun. The game was called at sundown, the score 1–1. Inning after inning, each player strove to drive in the run that would break the stalemate. Neither players nor umpire asked for mercy. Trusting one another to hit hard, field clean, and call them right, they weren't disappointed—not with Amanda Clement in charge of the game.

"'If every game in the National and American Leagues were umpired by women, the one objectionable feature of baseball would be forever removed.' So spoke Miss Amanda Clement . . . who has won distinction the last two years as the original girl umpire.

"'Can you suggest a single reason why all the baseball umpires should not be women?' she queried. 'Of course you can't. I mean just what I say, seriously, that all the official baseball umpires of the country should be women.

"'It certainly will not be disputed that the only objection that is found in this day to baseball is rowdyism. In spite of fines and rules and all, ball players will scrap with the umpire, and the public doesn't like that. Then, again, the crowd itself will often spoil a game by continually roasting the umpire. The umpire himself gets rattled, probably, and doesn't know but that he has been favoring one of the teams and tries to square himself. And then he finds himself in more trouble.

"'Now if women were umpiring none of this would happen. Do you suppose any ball player in the country would step up to a good-looking girl and say to her, "you color-blind, pickle-brained, cross-eyed idiot, if you don't stop throwing the soup into me I'll distribute your features all over your countenance!" Of course he wouldn't. Ball players aren't a bad lot. In fact, my experience is that they have more than the usual allowance of chivalry. And I don't believe there's anybody in the country, unless it's Muggsy McGraw, that would speak rudely to a woman umpire even if he thought his drive was "safe a mile" instead of foul.

"'Then there's the crowd. There's a good deal of cowardliness about the roasting of umpires by crowds, because hardly any of the fans that shout all sorts of insults from the bleachers would have the nerve to say anything of the kind to the umpire's face. . . .'"

—*The Cincinnati Enquirer,* circa 1906

Alta Weiss

Alta Weiss, age seventeen, in her early
pitching apparel

THE OVERWHELMING MAJORITY OF WOMEN WHO PLAYED
baseball at the turn of the century came from the working class or
the farm. Alta Weiss, born February 9, 1890, the second of three
daughters, did not. Her father, Dr. George Weiss, was a respected
physician in Ragersville, Ohio, who indulged his daughter's love
of sports and once confessed that he had only two hobbies—his
Holstein cattle and his baseball-pitching daughter, Alta. In 1905,
Dr. Weiss established a local high school so that Alta could play
on its baseball team. He also built Weiss Ball Park, where she
played on the town's younger "second" team.

According to Ragersville legend, Alta Weiss was born to pitch:
at age two she hurled corncobs at the family cat with wrist-snap
and follow-through; at age fourteen she was pitching and playing
first base for the town's "second" team. John Berger, who worked
as Dr. Weiss's handyman and hostler, played third base on the
same team. "She had a man's windup then and good speed,"
recalled Berger, who added that she was fiercely competitive.
When she first began to play, some infielders would simply lob
the ball to her. "Come on," she would shout, "put some sting on
it! Do you want him to beat it out?" Still, it must have seemed

unlikely that Alta Weiss would become a star pitcher for a semi-pro team. But when the opportunity arrived, she seized it.

In August 1907, the Weiss family was vacationing in Vermilion, a Lake Erie resort town. There, Alta approached a group of young men and asked to play catch with them. Perhaps they were amused, perhaps chivalrous. But when their gloves stopped smoking and their hands stopped stinging, they were in awe.

The mayor of the town promptly suggested to the manager of the semipro Vermilion Independents that he should sign a seventeen-year-old, long-haired player who wore a skirt. The manager wanted nothing to do with women who played baseball, so the mayor arranged for a game between two local teams, with Alta pitching for one of them. Striking out fifteen men in that game, Alta set the large crowd buzzing about her skill. Straight-away, the manager of the Independents changed his mind and asked the young pitcher to join his team.

She agreed. Wearing a long blue skirt in her first semipro game, she pitched five innings, giving up four hits and one run. For the remainder of the eleven-inning game, she played first base. The Independents won, 4–3.

Throughout northeast Ohio, news of the "Girl Wonder" spread fast. During the remainder of the 1907 season, Alta Weiss pitched seven more games for the Independents, attracting more than thirteen thousand people. Special trains carried fans to the ball-parks to see her. When the Independents challenged the Vacha All-Stars of Cleveland to a game, big-city residents flocked to see the Ragersville hero. For her appearance in League Park, Cleveland's major league stadium, the Girl Wonder received

"It's a little indelicate to say it, but I had also learned to throw a spitball. I chewed gum during a game, to make sure I had an abundance of saliva. For a girl, I had a pretty fair fast ball and I had control except with the knuckler and spitter. I never knew how they would break."

—Alta Weiss

"Dear Mama: I am having a fine time only am getting pretty tired of heat. I am making a lot of money. Ha! My blue skirt is about all in and my others are all too short. I played ball in my blue one. I will write one of these days. A kiss. Alta."

—Postcard of August 22, 1907

Weiss, age eighteen, after she switched
to bloomers

$100, a hefty amount of money for a semipro. With Alta on the mound, Vermilion won, 7–6.

Watching the husky five-foot, six-inch rookie pitch, a reporter for the *Cleveland Press* wrote, "She is there with chimes and bells. In the second inning she showed up best. She struck out the first batter. The next man drove a sizzling liner at her. She made a catch that increased the cheers threefold. It was a beauty that would do credit to any pitcher. Then she fanned the next batter, retiring the side." Alta's record for the months of September and October was 5–3.

During the off-season of 1907–1908, Dr. Weiss had a heated gymnasium built on his property so that his daughter could pitch to John Berger all winter long. Alta and her father agreed that she

During her days of retirement, Dr. Alta Weiss sat on her porch and watched a young girl play baseball down the street. Lois Youngen's uncles had both played ball with Alta, and one of them had been her catcher. One day Dr. Weiss summoned Lois to her porch, gave her lemonade, and asked her about her ballplaying, how she hit and fielded.

At the end of the visit, Alta presented Lois with a baseball. "She said it was autographed by Babe Ruth. I don't know if it really was Ruth's signature or not. If it was, he had the best handwriting for a man I've ever seen. It might have been some sort of promotional piece. But Alta signed the other side of it. It's her signature, I know, because I witnessed it. I still have the baseball."

Like Alta Weiss, Lois Youngen also went on to play professional baseball, becoming a catcher for the Fort Wayne Daisies of the All-American Girls Baseball League. Looking back on her conversation with Alta Weiss, she realizes she was in the presence of a pioneer.

should work out with weights all winter, too. One newspaper reported that "the muscles of her small forearm and her biceps are like steel."

Early in 1908, Dr. Weiss purchased a semipro team, naming it the Weiss All-Stars. That spring, the Ragersville High School commencement date was changed so that Alta could graduate on a date that didn't conflict with one of her All-Star pitching engagements. When she took the mound for her new team, she wore bloomers rather than a cumbersome skirt.

Touring Ohio and Kentucky, the Weiss All-Stars played to record crowds of appreciative fans, many of whom tossed money onto the infield after particularly good plays. Because she was the star attraction, Alta pitched five innings of every game, then played first base. Every evening, one of her sisters would rub Alta's pitching arm with arnica, a plant extract used to treat sprains and bruises.

PHYSICAL CONDITIONING

Today, nearly a century after Alta Weiss pitched in League Park, most people still don't believe that women can throw well. Dr. Fred Stransky, current director of the Meadow Brook Health Enhancement Institute in Michigan, asserts otherwise. "Men and women do have tremendous differences in upper body strength," he agrees. "But their lower body strength is almost equal, and most of the velocity and strength in pitching is related to leg strength. Leg strength is critical, and from that perspective, women are not at a disadvantage at all. The only reason women don't throw as well as men is because of physical conditioning. They haven't been given the opportunity to develop these abilities."

Pitcher Alta Weiss, seated, Irma Weiss, standing

Alta Weiss

While reporters who covered her second season were generally enthusiastic, a few looked at weaknesses as well as strengths. The *Messenger-Graphic* informed readers that Alta "fields well, handling bunts with ease and gets the ball away fast and to the proper place when she gets hold of it." But "at bat she is not so much. Usually she pushes the bat toward the ball, ungracefully and without force. . . ." Possibly Weiss was ahead of her time, a natural for the designated-hitter American League, in which pitchers do not bat at all.

After the summer of 1908, the young pitcher attended the Wooster Academy in preparation for college. Two years later she entered the Starling College of Medicine in Columbus (now Ohio State University Medical College). During these years she played some baseball, but after 1910 her pitching appearances were infrequent. In 1914 she graduated as a Doctor of Medicine, the only female in the class.

During World War I, young Dr. Weiss took over the practice of an enlisted doctor in Sugarcreek, Ohio, and in 1925 she set up a medical practice in Norwalk, Ohio. In 1927 she married Ragersville resident and service station owner John E. Hisrich. After twelve years of marriage, Alta and John separated, and in 1946, when George Weiss died, Alta moved back to Ragersville to take over her father's medical practice. Eventually she retired and became something of a recluse, sitting on the porch all summer, reading newspapers and watching Ragersville youngsters play ball. Dr. Weiss died February 12, 1964.

Lizzie Murphy

AT AGE NINETEEN, MARY ELIZABETH MURPHY HAD HER
own listing in the Warren, Rhode Island, directory. The year was
1913: women wore ground-skimming skirts, weren't permitted to
vote in most states, and seldom dared to be more than wives,
mothers, and housekeepers. For Lizzie Murphy, there was no dare
about it—she simply *was* what the directory specified: "ball player."

One of six children of an Irish mill worker and a French-
Canadian mother, she was born April 13, 1894, and grew up
playing baseball with her brother Henry. Their father, himself a
ballplayer, encouraged them both. While Lizzie was a fast runner, good soccer player, and great swimmer and ice hockey player,
it was baseball that drew her. Soon she was the first chosen by
local team captains.

At age twelve, she went to work in the woolens mill, but she
spent much of her time "dreaming of the outdoors and baseball."
After work and on weekends, she played the game she loved. By
age fifteen she had earned a spot on several amateur teams, including the Silk Hats and the Warren Baseball Club.

Once, she questioned whether she should continue. "I about
decided that baseball wasn't a game for a girl and that I'd quit,"

"She has a fine pair of hands, baseball
hands. The fingers are straight, strong and
supple. The knuckles are normal, attest-
ing to her ability to catch a ball in the
palm, not the finger tips."

—Barney Madden, reporter for the
Providence Journal, 1944

she explained. "But then I went to watch one of the games and got so excited I couldn't stay out. When I see a batter swinging wild or stepping back from the ball it makes me crazy to take a turn at the plate and line one out." That hunger to hit one out couldn't be denied: Lizzie Murphy chose baseball.

In Warren she was offered money to play for a semipro team—$5 a game plus a share of the take (collected by passing around a hat). When word went out that a woman would start at first base, attendance swelled: $85 was collected from the crowd. But the manager went back on his word and failed to pay his first baseman or give her a share of the collection. Next week, Murphy showed up for practice, but when the time came to depart for Newport, she refused to board the bus. Her one-woman players' strike won her what she deserved: the manager thereafter paid her $5 a game and an equal share of the receipts.

Maturing as a player, Lizzie left the Warren teams to sign with the Providence Independents, an important step upward. In 1918 she signed a contract with Ed Carr, owner of a semipro team called Ed Carr's All-Stars of Boston (sometimes called the Boston All-Stars). The jubilant owner informed reporters, "No ball is too hard for her to scoop out of the dirt, and when it comes to batting, she packs a mean wagon tongue."

In her early days, Murphy wore bloomers and played with her long reddish-brown hair flowing loose. With the All-Stars her hair was braided and tucked under her cap, and she wore the regular baseball uniform of the day: a peaked cap, heavy wool shirt, wide belt, baggy pants, thick stockings and stirrups, and glove. The only difference between her uniform and that of the men was that hers had LIZZIE MURPHY stitched across the front and back—so that everybody would know that the first baseman making sensational plays was, in fact, the woman they came to see.

"Spike" Murphy, as she was sometimes called, was such a drawing card that Carr featured a picture of her on his stationery. When some criticized him for exploiting a young woman who (they presumed) couldn't really play hardball, he retorted: "She swells attendance, and she's worth every cent I pay her. But most important, she produces the goods."

With the All-Stars, Lizzie played one hundred games a summer up and down the states and provinces of New England and eastern Canada. Chances are she was worth a lot more than every cent Carr paid her. Like her fellow ballplayers, she needed to supplement her income and did so by selling autographed pictures of herself in the stands between innings. In later years she recalled with fondness places such as Dorchester, Massachusetts, where she once sold $50 worth of cards at a game, and with less excitement cities such as Worcester, Massachusetts, where she sold only $22 worth.

On the field, Spike played the game with intensity. At first base, she chattered, always talking it up to build morale among her teammates. A reporter once asked whether her teammates swore within her earshot. "Of course they cursed and swore," she replied, "but I didn't mind. I knew all the words myself."

It wasn't common knowledge, but she was fluent in French. In Quebec she once listened in as the opposing first-base coach discussed the steal sign with a player. Not letting on that she understood, Lizzie called time after a few minutes and set up her own

The photo that Lizzie Murphy sold to fans

Warren Walden, secretary of the Rhode Island Amateur Baseball Association, related that Lizzie Murphy once told him with pride that she had singled off the great Satchel Paige during a barnstorming game. After the game, a sportswriter asked Negro League catcher Josh Gibson if Satchel had softened up on the pitch to Lizzie. Gibson replied that Satchel was bearing down with everything he had because he didn't want to be charged with a hit by a woman of any color.

signal with the catcher. When the steal was on, she would flash the catcher a sign and he would be ready. "Nailed five of them that way," she remembered proudly.

Carr's team often included former major-leaguers in the lineup. Murphy fit right in, proud of her place on the team. "I was always rough and ready, and I could take it," she explained. "I got in shape beating rugs and chopping wood. This kept me fit for running the bases and driving the ball to the outfield." For seventeen years, from 1918 to 1935, she earned her living playing the game. New Englanders dubbed her the Queen of Baseball.

In 1922, when the Boston Red Sox sponsored a charity game (the Sox against a group of American League and New England All-Stars), Lizzie Murphy was chosen as the All-Star first baseman. There in Fenway Park, the team's third baseman decided to test her mettle. When a Sox batter hit a hard grounder his way, the third baseman fielded it . . . and held it. At the last possible moment, he gunned the ball across the diamond. Never shrinking, Murphy caught the bullet and the runner was out. Walking over to the shortstop, the third baseman nodded in the direction of first. "She'll do," he said.

Six years after that incident, Lizzie played another major league exhibition game, this one with the National League All-Stars, against the Boston Braves. The first woman to play for a major league team in an exhibition game (Babe Didrikson would become the second in 1934), she is reported to have been the first person to play with both American League and National League All-Star teams. In addition, she played first base for the

Cleveland Colored Giants of the Negro Leagues in a game at Rocky Point, Rhode Island.

At age forty-one, Murphy retired from baseball. She then cleaned houses for a living, worked in a spinning mill, and did the hard, wet labor of quahogging and clamming. Although she married in 1937, her husband, Walter Larivee, died a few years later, and once again Lizzie was on her own. Hers is the story of many a ballplayer of the time: poorly paid, little or no retirement income, forced to work hard all her life for food and shelter. Like many another ballplayer, she had a fierce and stubborn pride: if it hurt, she didn't show it. On July 27, 1964, Lizzie Murphy died at the age of seventy.

The Western Bloomer Girls

Nelson as pitcher for Olson's Cherokee

Indian team, 1908

THOUGH ONLY THIRTY YEARS OLD IN 1911, MAUD NELSON was a baseball veteran. Her fourteen years of baseball experience, ten of them in the company of her husband, John B. Olson, Jr., shaped her decisions on owning and managing, so that when she formed the Western Bloomer Girls, it was with full knowledge of what she wanted. She made no mistakes: the Western Bloomer Girls, her first team, were a huge success.

Like all of her teams to come, the Western Bloomer Girls bore a distinctive Nelson stamp: seven traits that, in combination, set them apart from other teams. Three of these features were based on practices that Olson had implemented with his barnstormers, the Cherokee Indian Base Ball Club. First, Nelson sought out a co-owner. Just as Olson owned the Cherokee club in partnership with F. McMillan or L. C. Figg, she owned the Westerns in partnership not only with her husband, but also with Kate Becker, a fellow ballplayer from Chicago. On a co-owned team, both risk and profits are shared: such an organization is more likely to survive tough times than is one with a single owner. Formed in February 1911, the Western Bloomer Girls practiced in April and started

Left: The Western Bloomer Girls: Nelson, seated, far left

Below: Ad from the *Watervliet Record,* April 12, 1912

A Great Attraction!
BASE BALL!

THE WELL KNOWN

WESTERN
BLOOMER GIRLS

BASE BALL CLUB

Will play the Watervliet Club at their new
NEW BASE BALL PARK IN WATERVLIET,

Saturday, April 27, at 2 p.m.

The only opportunity you will get this year
of seeing the Girls in action in the Great
National Game. Come and see the famous
girl pitcher, Maud Nelson.

ADMISSION 25 CENTS.

their tour in May, with Nelson pitching and playing third base and Becker pitching and playing second.

"Get their attention" was another cue that Maud took from John. Though Olson was usually thought of as a baseball man, he always considered himself a carnival man and acted accordingly. In 1907 he arranged for a ten-piece Indian band to tour with the Cherokee club and two years later hired "the tallest man in the world" to walk the streets with a sandwich board on game days.

Maud preferred to achieve the same goals with more subtlety, to travel light, and to keep the overhead down. Instead of touring with musicians, she would hire a local band to meet the bloomers at the train station. Oompah-pah-ing its way down the main streets, the marching band was followed by the bat-and-glove-toting ballplayers, resplendent in professional uniforms. "It was a wonderful tradition," says Margaret Gisolo, who played for

"At bat the Bloomers displayed signal ability. They wielded the club with all the agility and fearlessness of professionals, and scored more hits than a number of the masculine teams that have opposed Hartford this year.

"It was the first game in which the locals have engaged at the Hartford park where they found themselves without the support of the fans. The girls were plainly the favorites and received the applause for their clever plays."

—*The Hartford Daily Spring,*
September 27, 1911

Postcard of Western Bloomer Girls: Maud Nelson, seated, second from left

Nelson's last team, "and it worked." Swept up by the music and the challenge, happy crowds followed the parade to the ballpark.

A third recognizable trait of all Nelson teams was that they were composed of very good ballplayers. John had established this pattern with the Cherokee Indian team (composed entirely of Native Americans, though not necessarily of Cherokees) and Maud, herself a great ballplayer, would never have settled for mediocrity. Despite the existence of hundreds of bloomer girl teams during the period 1890-1935, her teams were world-renowned. In 1925, half a world away in Japan, playing with the Philadelphia Bobbies, former major-leaguer Eddie Ainsmith told the press that in the United States there were only two outstanding bloomer teams—the one from Chicago (Maud Nelson's) and the one from New York (Margaret Nabel's).

Because they were so good, the Western Bloomer Girls were immensely popular. In 1912 they faced the Watervliet, Michigan, team on opening day in the town's brand new ballpark, and the crowd turned out to be the largest of the season. As they toured Indiana and Michigan, the Westerns drew sizable crowds (in June in Detroit they played before seventy-two hundred fans) because they played exciting, heads-up baseball.

Although she borrowed techniques from John and others, Maud did things her own way in several areas, starting with recruitment. Most bloomer teams, such as the later New York Bloomer Girls and Philadelphia Bobbies, confined their recruiting bases to their home cities and surrounding areas. Not so with Nelson teams. From the beginning, Maud found her players in both city and country. The Westerns, for example, were composed of local

Michigan players such as Ruth Woods (a pitcher capable of hitting home runs) and Mabel Bowers, as well as of Chicagoans such as Kate Becker.

In later years, Nelson would expand recruiting efforts across the entire country. Besides being highly respected, gregarious, and well liked, she was an unusually good scout with an amazing number of contacts: people wrote to her from all over, excitedly informing her about good local players. Often she arranged playing dates so that the barnstormers could swing through a particular town and pick up a new ballplayer, male or female: that's how she signed Rose Gacioch in 1934. This combination of a broad base and many contacts helped Nelson build her first team and her last, and every one in between.

Another distinctive feature of Nelson's teams was that they seldom played night games. In those days, many barnstormers carried portable lighting in order to draw fans with the novelty. On his railroad car, "Clementine," John Olson had a special under-compartment built to hold the baseball equipment; grandstands that would seat one thousand people; a twelve-hundred-foot-long, twelve-foot-high canvas fence (to shut out freeloaders); and a complete lighting plant for night games. Because of the primitive lighting systems of those days, night games were played with a larger, softer ball and shorter basepaths. The Cherokees played such games in 1908 and the American Athletic Girls as late as 1929. But not the Western Bloomer Girls. Maud Nelson loved hardball and day games, and although her later teams would play night games if that's what a town offered, she doesn't seem to have carried lighting with her.

"Some of you may remember my playing in Georgia in 1914. I was with the Western Bloomers, an all-woman team, and we played the crack Macon club, and beat 'em, too. So you see women playing baseball are not so novel after all, and we do not consider ourselves subjects for the zoo."

—Elizabeth "Fargo" Pull, captain of the Hollywood Movie Girls Baseball Team, Atlanta, September, 1930

Blue, white, and sepia-toned poster, now a collector's item

The Westerns stood out from other bloomer teams in still another way: six women and three men took the field. Many early bloomer teams played with one man, others with five or six men disguised as women. Nelson almost always played three men. As manager, she put them at catcher, shortstop, and center field, but occasionally she called upon a man to pitch, in which case the entire outfield would consist of women. In later years, she would go beyond simply fielding three men: she would develop a strategy for placing the men in the batting order.

Finally, Maud Nelson differed from other bloomer owners in that after she started a team, made it competitive, and made it famous . . . she then sold it to her co-owner. Once sold, most Nelson teams continued to thrive: the Western Bloomer Girls, which she sold to Kate Becker in October 1912 after two full seasons of play, were still going strong ten years later; and the American Athletic Girls, her second team, played on for many years after being sold to original co-owner Rose Figg.

This last step in the Nelson pattern is critically important to the history of women in baseball. By creating teams that continued to flourish, she significantly increased the opportunities for women to play. With the exception of those who stuck to the New York Bloomer Girls for life, almost every adventurous female ballplayer relied on one or another of Nelson's teams in order to earn a living.

Part 2

THE
BOLD
YEARS

IN 1920, THREE YEARS AFTER MAUD NELSON LEFT
Watervliet for Chicago, the Black Sox scandal shocked the public
and shook major league owners. With "the fix" dominating sports
headlines, owners appointed federal judge Kenesaw Mountain
Landis as baseball's first commissioner—a figure of moral authority who would clean up the game and thus assure that ticket
money would continue to roll in. In addition to a $50,000 salary,
Landis received complete authority to rule baseball (excluding
on-field rules).

With Landis at its helm, major league baseball sailed through
the Roaring Twenties. The game became more popular than ever:
in 1920 attendance topped six million, and two years later ex-
ceeded nine million. Neither presidents nor movie stars were photo-
graphed as often as was Babe Ruth. The Sultan of Swat electrified
fans by hitting an unheard-of twenty-nine home runs in 1919
and then, in 1920, almost doubling that figure to fifty-four. And
Ruth was far from the only baseball hero of the decade: Lou
Gehrig, Rogers Hornsby, Hack Wilson, George Sisler, and Harry
Heilmann were just a few of the many in the national spotlight.

A surging economy led to increased advertising for consumer
spending on automobiles, radios, clothes, and canned foods, as
well as increased recreational spending on movies and sporting
events. Branch Rickey, general manager of the St. Louis Cardinals, used the owners' money to buy a different kind of commodity:
minor league baseball teams. In this way, Rickey helped develop
a so-called farm system that supplied the Cardinals with experienced young players. In New York, the owners of the pinstriped

sluggers built what they couldn't buy—the new and elegant Yankee Stadium.

Although anybody with ticket money could attend a game in Yankee Stadium, not everybody with talent was permitted to play. But those whom organized baseball excluded from the field took action. In 1920, Andrew "Rube" Foster, owner of the Chicago American Giants, created the Negro National League to help black owners and players gain control over the money that flowed through the turnstiles. Over the next thirty years some of the best ballplayers of all time—stars such as Satchel Paige, Josh Gibson, Turkey Stearns, Pop Lloyd, and Cool Papa Bell—thrilled legions of fans.

During the bold years, female baseball players also forged ahead. Margaret Nabel took over the New York Bloomer Girls in 1920, making them the predominant bloomer team of the East Coast. In the Midwest, Maud Nelson clad her players in standard baseball uniforms and dropped the "bloomer" designation altogether, calling her first team of the 1920s the All-Star Athletic Girls. Mary O'Gara took the Philadelphia Bobbies to Japan, where they challenged men's college teams. And fourteen-year-old Margaret Gisolo joined the nation-wide American Legion Junior Baseball program in 1928. A solid hitter, speedy base-stealer, and superb second baseman, she helped lead the Blanford Cubs to the Indiana state title.

The boom days looked as if they would never end, but the bust came soon enough, and with it a rowdier type of baseball, exemplified by the Gas House Gang of the St. Louis Cardinals, with their daring base-stealing and on-field brawls. Baseball attendance passed the ten-million mark in 1930, but it fell to six million in 1933 and didn't work its way back until 1940. Desperate to continue making money, major league owners found themselves turning to the very things they had opposed for decades. Night baseball had been introduced by bloomer girl teams at the turn of the century and adopted by most semipro teams by 1930. Yet major league baseball refused to introduce night games until 1935. Imitating the minors, the majors began to offer more "promotion" nights and interesting challenges—in 1934, Olympic hero Babe Didrikson pitched exhibition games for the Cardinals, the Athletics, and the Indians. There was even consistent talk of racial integration as a way of drawing more fans and making more money, but Commissioner Landis, who died in office in 1944, staunchly resisted integration.

Down in the minors, owners and managers made bold moves of their own. In Missouri in 1931 the manager of the Joplin Miners invited a young woman, Vada Corbus, to try out for catcher; in Arkansas in 1936 the manager of the Fayetteville Bears played a woman, Sonny Dunlap, for an entire game. Perhaps the boldest of the bold was Joe Engel, who in 1931 signed young Virne Beatrice "Jackie" Mitchell to an official minor league contract for the Chattanooga Lookouts. She pitched in an exhibition game against the New York Yankees on April 2, 1931, and struck out Babe Ruth and Lou Gehrig.

That same year, Edith Houghton played on the Hollywood Girls, who toured Texas and Oklahoma, competing against minor league teams. Likewise, Maud Nelson's last team, the All Star

Ranger Girls, challenged Class D teams in the early 1930s. During the bold years, women reached out for more—for international tours, junior baseball, and minor league contracts.

In the mid-1930s, however, bloomer girl baseball, which had lasted for nearly half a century, gave way to softball—a game significantly less expensive and less difficult to play. No national organization promoted baseball for women, whereas groups such as the YWCA, Catholic Youth Organization, National Recreation Association, Amateur Softball Association, and National Softball Association all supported softball for women. Three generations of ballplayers who had played the real thing watched in dismay as corporations and communities everywhere pushed women into softball. By 1940 it must have looked to the entire nation as if women never had and never would play baseball.

Margaret Nabel and the New York Bloomer Girls

"Margaret Nabel was a heavy woman; not fat, but built solidly. She was a businesswoman, very much so. Nobody could put anything over on her. When we got money, it was all split up and that was it. We had traveling expenses and other expenses that were paid for us. She was a congenial person, but a businesswoman. She knew what she was doing.

"She was a good manager, very good to the girls who played for her. Of course we didn't have contracts like they have now."

—Ella Birmingham, former New York
Bloomer Girl

ON THE EAST COAST, MARGARET NABEL WAS AS important as Maud Nelson was in the Midwest—and better known, for Nabel managed only one team, the famous New York Bloomer Girls. The environment of Staten Island, Nabel's disciplinarian character, and her flair for promotion all went into the making and shaping of the "female champions of the world."

Born in Perth Amboy, New Jersey, on August 27, 1896, one of seven children, young Margaret grew up on Staten Island. The island was supplying ballplayers to the major leagues by the 1880s, and by 1900 companies were sponsoring baseball teams at every shipbuilding dock. In 1928 there were 250 baseball teams on the island, four teams for every square mile of land. The national pastime was played by children, women, and men.

In this hotbed of baseball, three old-time local players (Dan Whalen, Joe Manning, and Eddie Manning) formed the New York Bloomer Girls in 1910. Although the team was late in getting started (A. P. Gibbs was touring with his Ohio-based bloomers in 1892, and Maud Nelson was pitching for the Boston Bloomer Girls in 1897), it lasted without interruption until the end of the bloomer era.

Young Margaret Nabel graduated from Curtis High School in 1914, a member of the baseball, field hockey, tennis, and rifle teams. That year, Pat Kelly, a catcher for the semipro Siscos, asked her to pitch for his team against the New York Bloomer Girls, and she accepted. Years later she recalled her relative lack of success in that first outing: "I had poor Pat jumping all over the place, catching my slants, and the eight bases on balls I handed out sure do not speak well for my control in that game." Toward the end of that 1914 season, Margaret joined the New York Bloomer Girls.

A pitcher when need be, as well as an occasional outfielder, Nabel gained real fame as a manager. In 1920, before she was twenty-five years old, she took over the New York Bloomer Girls and barnstormed from Nova Scotia to Florida, challenging men's company-sponsored teams. From then on the team was referred to as Margaret Nabel and the New York Bloomer Girls.

Unlike Maud Nelson, Nabel built her team on a narrow basis: Staten Island and its environs. But that area happened to be rich with talented ballplayers. Of the New York Bloomer Girls, Margaret Nabel and Helen Demarest were from the island; Maggie Riley, Ethel Condon, and Toots Andres were from what is now Queens; and Nina "Babe" McCuttun was from Brooklyn, Elsie Ruhnke from Newark, Florrie O'Rourke from Manhattan, and Hattie Michaels from Bayonne, New Jersey. On the rare occasion that she ran out of New York and New Jersey players, Nabel recruited Philadelphia players such as Mary Gilroy and Edith Houghton to play for a game, a series, or a season.

Nabel's character molded her players into a disciplined unit.

"It is comparatively difficult to locate, develop and retain capable and reliable girl players, as you can well imagine. Sometimes the parents object and sometimes it's a steady boy friend; ofttimes the girls are too young, they wish to remain strictly amateur, or they tire of steady play.

"Players are strictly disciplined, as we cannot tolerate looseness of any kind.

"Against all this, it was interesting to note that in our series last fall with the Philadelphia Bobbies, there were five girls on our club who have been members of the New York Bloomer Girls for 15 or more years. . . .

"We allow absolutely no drinking nor carousing, and we all observe a regular big-league curfew at 11. In addition, players must write home at least once a week. . . ."

—Margaret Nabel, *The Staten Island Advance*, April 4, 1931

Before she joined them, the New York Bloomer Girls were a rowdy bunch, gaining notoriety in 1913 when they trashed a hotel in Raleigh, North Carolina—breaking windows, mirrors, and chairs, and beating back the police with bats and balls. No such behavior was tolerated by Manager Nabel. According to Joe Venditti, an Islander who played against her, she ran the Bloomer Girls with an iron fist. Ella Birmingham, who played for her, says she was very strict. And Ralph diStasio, who as a high school student frequented Nabel's candy store in the 1930s, remembers her as being "very demanding of the schoolchildren. There was no loitering tolerated in the store, no profanity. It was a well-operated business. The schoolchildren toed the line, or they didn't come into the store once they were out of her good graces. She was very military, and she didn't take guff from anybody."

While strict, Nabel was fair. Ella Birmingham remembers that any money collected was immediately divided among the players. Ralph diStasio, returning from World War II as a twenty-three-year-old veteran, bought the candy store from Margaret and her partner, Helen Demarest. "They were good, fine people," he says, "who treated us well when we took over the store."

By all accounts, Nabel was a tough businesswoman. If a town didn't have a fence to shut out freeloaders, she would insist that a portable one be erected. If the New York Bloomer Girls weren't paid their agreed-upon share before the game started, she pulled the players off the field. No unscrupulous or untrustworthy promoters could take her in, and she must have considered it extreme gullibility or incredible folly that Mary O'Gara and the Philadelphia Bobbies, who toured Japan in 1925, were stuck in that nation for weeks because their promoter pulled out and left them without funds to return home.

On the field as well as off, Nabel had strong ideas on how a bloomer team should operate. The New York Bloomer Girls originally consisted of seven women and two men, the latter playing catcher and shortstop. When Margaret took over, she continued the 7:2 ratio, but she believed strongly—at least at first—that the men should constitute the battery. In 1921 she told a reporter that the New York Bloomer Girls "use a male battery exclusively, as we feel that no female player can do justice to the pitcher's burden, and you will agree that the catching job belongs to a man, too." Yet within two years of her announcement about the hurling job belonging to a man, she had Helen Demarest and Ethel Condon pitching for the Bloomer Girls, particularly against other

The New York Bloomer Girls

women's teams. Possibly she sensed that fans would consider it unfair for one bloomer team to use a male pitcher when the other one didn't.

Margaret Nabel's flair for promotion certainly helped shape the "female champions of the world." In previous decades, many bloomer teams had used as advertisements postcards with the team photo on front and a lineup scorecard on back. The Star Bloomers had such postcards, as did the Western Bloomer Girls. Teams undoubtedly sold these cards at baseball games to bring in more revenue. When Margaret was a player on the New York Bloomer Girls, the postcards pictured the entire lineup—seven

Postcard of Margaret Nabel (far right) and the New York Bloomer Girls

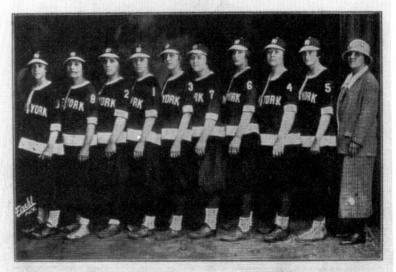

NEW YORK BLOOMER GIRLS, Inc. Margaret R. Nabel, Manager
Address—50 Beach Street, Stapleton, Staten Island, N. Y.

Left to Right—9. Ethel Condon; 8. Edna Kouri; 2. Toots Andres; 1. Helen Demarest, Capt.; 3. Mae Knapesek; 7. "Hack" McCuttun; 6. Elsie Ruhnke; 4. Florrie O'Rourke; 5. Gean Whalen. Margaret Nabel, Manager.

women and two men. After Nabel became manager, however, the postcards featured only female players, giving the New York Bloomer Girls a distinctive look.

Postcards weren't her only means of promotion. Nabel went out of her way to give newspaper interviews. She also coined slogans such as "In existence since 1910 and still going strong," thus conveying the solidity and success of the Bloomer Girls. Perhaps the best publicity of all, though, was the fact that the New York Bloomer Girls were very good ballplayers, giving the best of teams a close game. Along the eastern seaboard, Nabel's team was so well known and so highly rated that it became the highest ambition of many town and semipro players to beat Margaret Nabel and the New York Bloomer Girls.

The postcards, the interviews, the schedules—all these things Nabel would plan in advance. But she was also a master of seizing the moment and running with it. If an opportunity for making money came her way, she grabbed it.

In Philadelphia, working-class women played factory-sponsored baseball. Young Mary Gilroy played for such a team, the Fleisher Bloomer Girls, and after she married she played for athletic club teams such as the Philadelphia Girls A.C. Aware of the opportunities Philadelphia offered, Nabel took the New York Bloomer Girls there as early as 1923, to challenge women's teams as well as men's. On September 9, 1923, the Bloomer Girls played against the Philadelphia Girls A.C. in the neutral territory of Brooklyn. Conceived of and promoted by Nabel, the game was billed as part of "a series to decide the female championship of the East." (Later, she would up the ante to "female championship

In praising the longevity of her team, Nabel once told a reporter that she had seen many female baseball clubs come and go, including:

The Boston Bloomer Girls

The Quaker City Girls

The Fleisher Yarn Girls of Philadelphia

The Troy Collar League Girls

The General Electric Girls of Schenectady

The Philadelphia A.C. Girls

The Wilmington Rubber League Girls

The Eastman Kodak Girls of Rochester

The Stetson Bloomer Girls of Philadelphia

The Baltimore Black Sox Colored Girls

The Heath Silk Girls of Scranton

of the world.") In that game, Helen Demarest pitched for the Bloomers, who walloped the Philadelphia team, 21–13.

But it was the Philadelphia Bobbies, a bloomer team managed by Mary O'Gara, that Margaret Nabel most often challenged to "the world championship"—and then, because the Bloomers won each and every game, Nabel labeled the New York Bloomer Girls "the undisputed female champions of the world."

Although it was more profitable to play close to home, Nabel didn't hesitate to travel if an opportunity was big enough. In April 1931, after Jackie Mitchell's minor league contract was voided by Commissioner Kenesaw Mountain Landis, Nabel immediately offered the young southpaw a contract to pitch for the New York Bloomer Girls. After Mitchell turned down the offer and went instead with the Lookout Juniors, a men's team, Nabel marched the Bloomers into the state of Tennessee (where they had never ventured before) and challenged Jackie and the Juniors to a big game. The two teams played before a sellout crowd on May 30, 1931, in Chattanooga's minor league stadium.

Jackie and the Juniors won that encounter, 7–4, but the gracious Southern crowd appreciated the "Yorkers." The *Chattanooga Daily Times* reported: "Condon, star pitcher for the visitors, showed the fans some real tossing. The crowd rose to its feet to applaud her as she struck out Bill Wells [Lookout slugger] with a man on third base. Ginger Robinson, another member of the famous girls' team, played fine ball at the hot corner. She pulled a base hit out of the air to keep the Lookouts from scoring."

Nabel's march into Tennessee was bold—but it was also a sign of changing times. By 1931 the environment she relied upon had changed. The boom days of the 1920s were gone, replaced by unemployment and shriveling attendance at baseball games. Baseball for women was being replaced by softball, which required less money, less space, and, overall, less talent. In 1932 Nabel had to advertise in the newspapers for local opponents: traveling in search of games was too risky financially. Still, the New York Bloomer Girls ended the year with a bang, defeating Edith Houghton's Philadelphia A.C. team before the largest crowd ever to witness a baseball game at the new Bayonne City Stadium.

At the end of the 1933 season, Nabel disbanded the team and bought the candy store across from Curtis High School, operating it until 1946. In 1957 she and her sister Dora moved to Hollywood, Florida. An entrepreneur until the end, Margaret bought and managed an apartment building. She died on September 30, 1967, and is buried in Florida. Today Staten Island regularly produces championship girls' softball teams, particularly from Curtis High School. Only a few old-timers, however, remember the glory days of Margaret Nabel and the New York Bloomer Girls.

MARY GILROY HOCKENBURY

Mary Gilroy was born in Philadelphia in 1903, the year of the first modern World Series and the prelude to the dead-ball era, when singles, bunts, and stolen bases brought in more runs than did slugging and yet the average baseball game was played in one hour and fifty-eight minutes.

With seven brothers and three sisters, Mary was a middle child. Six of her brothers played sports, particularly baseball. So did she. "There was not much else to do with six brothers," she jokes. The entire Gilroy family was sports-oriented. "Dad took all us kids to the games a lot." At the age of twelve Mary went to work, and in 1918 she was hired at Fleisher's, a yarn manufacturer. There she ran the balling machine and joined the factory-sponsored Fleisher Bloomer Girls. Nicknamed Scoops for her plays at first base, Gilroy played baseball for four years. A good hitter, she usually batted third or fourth. "We played two or three games a week," she says. "It was twilight ball, at five-thirty or six, after work."

The two most famous managers of women's barnstorming teams, Margaret Nabel and Maud Nelson, were both interested in Mary Gilroy. When the New York Bloomer Girls came into Philadelphia, Nabel often asked Scoops to play for the Yorkers. In January 1922, Gilroy received a letter from Maud Nelson Olson of Chicago, asking her if she would consider playing on a barnstorming team, for pay. Mary was about to turn nineteen. She stood five feet, seven inches tall and weighed 119 pounds.

Taking the train from Philadelphia to New Orleans, Gilroy linked up with Maud Olson and the Chicago All-Star Athletic Girls, training at Pelican Field, along with the New York Yankees. "The Yankees had the field from ten until twelve," remembers Mary, "then we had it from twelve until two, then they got it again at two." One day Babe Ruth walked up to the Chicago All-Stars and demanded, "Okay—who's the heavy hitter here?" The other players all pointed to Gilroy. So the Bambino posed with his arm around Mary's shoulders: the picture became one of her prized possessions.

After one season of barnstorming, Mary returned home and in 1923 married Bill Hockenbury, who had played on the Fleisher men's baseball team. Bill had been signed by the Philadelphia Athletics organization as a pitcher and had gone to Charlottesville to play Class A ball. But living conditions were poor and Bill was homesick: after a year he returned to Philadelphia, where he made more money playing sandlot baseball than he had in the minors.

Bill and Mary had seven children, five boys and two girls. That never stopped Mary from playing baseball. In Philadelphia she continued to play for local women's baseball teams, occasionally for the New York Bloomer Girls, and sometimes for a men's team such as the House of David when they came to town. Bill Hockenbury also played baseball regularly, for three or four different teams. And as the kids grew up, *they* played as well. "We ate and slept baseball," Mary recalls. "We'd get up from the dinner table and go to the ball game." Their closets were filled with the uniforms of different teams, and sometimes she wor-

ried that somebody would walk out the door wearing the wrong person's uniform, or the wrong team's uniform.

Three of the boys—Bill, Jim, and Tom—went on to play in the minor leagues, Bill as a third baseman, Jim as a first baseman, and Tom as a catcher. Of the three brothers, Bill (called Hock by his teammates) was in the minors the longest, from 1947 to 1958. An All-Star third baseman four out of six years, he played for Class A Savannah his first year, leading the league in homers and RBIs. Later Hock became a pitcher, then a coach.

Both Mary and Bill Hockenbury taught their children baseball skills. "It was fun," says Hock. "Mom would have a catch with us. It was great. The other kids in the neighborhood envied us." He believes that he and his brothers and sisters were more advanced in their skills because both parents played baseball with them.

When Hock was in the minor leagues during the 1950s, he would tell his teammates that his mother played baseball. They'd say, "Oh, you mean softball." He'd say, "No, I mean hardball." They

would say, "You mean softball." He would say, "No, I mean hardball." Finally he would give up mentioning it, because by the 1950s very few knew that women had played baseball.

"Mom" Hock, as she's called by those who know and respect her, knows that for her playing baseball was perfectly natural. "I'd rather play ball than eat," she declares. But she does believe that baseball isn't for every woman. "A lot of girls aren't capable of playing hardball. They're ladies. I was a tomboy. I could play baseball because I wasn't a lady. They couldn't." Thinking back on her barnstorming days and the men's teams she played against, she sees another reason why many women don't play baseball. "Men were nasty," she says. "They couldn't take women beating them. They didn't like it."

Edith Houghton and the Philadelphia Bobbies

PLAYING BASEBALL ALL DAY LONG WASN'T ENOUGH FOR young Edith Houghton. Indoors, she would rush into her parents' room and stare out the window. "You could see the diamond from my parents' bedroom window," she muses. "It was a sight to see."

Edith was born in Philadelphia on February 12, 1912, the youngest of ten children. Her love of baseball was encouraged by both her mother and her father. By age six she was playing hardball on the playgrounds and posing for portraits wearing a child-sized baseball suit. At eight she became the mascot of the Philadelphia police baseball teams, who regularly scheduled interdepartmental as well as intercity games. By now nicknamed the Kid, Edith would don her baseball uniform, shoulder her bat, and lead the police teams as they marched from the center-field flag pole to the plate. During the games she sat in the best seat, right next to the mayor of Philadelphia. By the time she was nine, the Kid was giving hitting, fielding, and throwing exhibitions before games.

Philadelphia at the time had two major league teams and a wealth of industrial baseball leagues, semipro leagues, city leagues, and amateur leagues—leagues for both men and women.

For employed working-class women, there were factory teams. For ballplaying girls and young women who didn't yet have jobs, the Philadelphia Bobbies were the team to join—so long as a player was willing to bob her hair. Started by Mary O'Gara in 1922, the Bobbies, unlike the New York Bloomer Girls, were composed of very young players, generally ranging in age from thirteen to twenty. And unlike Nabel, O'Gara almost never used male players.

The young and inexperienced Bobbies practiced on a Philadelphia playground. One day, ten-year-old Edith Houghton heard about them. "A boy told me there was a girls' baseball team out in Fairmont Park." Naturally the Kid headed for the diamond. "I knew one girl, Edith Ruth, who was playing. I had played against her at the playground. They put me at shortstop."

The ten-year-old starting shortstop was by far the youngest player on the team. Edith was so young that even the smallest cap and belt didn't fit her, so she tightened her navy blue cap with the block-letter B on the front with the aid of a safety pin in back, and with a pen knife she punched holes into her belt so it would hold up the uniform with "Bobbies" stitched across the front.

If the uniform was too big for Edith, the field wasn't. "She was all over that diamond," marvels former Bobbie teammate Loretta Jester Lipski. The Philadelphia sports reporters thought so, too, for they consistently praised the Kid's fielding and hitting. In one game against an adult team the ten-year-old went three for four. In another, she handled seven chances with only one error.

The Philadelphia papers did not lavish similar praise on the Bobbies, who lost one game to the Tinicum Bloomer Girls of Baltimore, 24–11, and another to the Lancaster (Pa.) Indians, a men's

Edith Houghton, age thirteen

team, 17–15—with the Indians batting left-handed the entire nine innings. But "little Miss Houghton, ten-year-old phenom, covered the ground at shortstop for the team and made herself a favorite with the fans by her splendid field work and ability at the bat."

In 1925 Mary O'Gara arranged for the Bobbies to tour Japan. During the Roaring Twenties there was a fair amount of baseball traffic between the United States and Japan: a team from the University of Chicago and two California teams composed of Japanese-Americans toured Japan around the same time the Bobbies did. According to O'Gara, her team had an agreement with Japanese sponsors to play fifteen games against men's college teams at $800 a game. With their parents' permission, twelve of the Bobbies (thirteen-year-old Edith Houghton included) boarded a Seattle-bound train on September 23. En route, they played eight scheduled games against men's town and semipro teams in places such as Fargo, North Dakota, and Whitefish, Montana.

In Seattle, new baseball uniforms awaited the Bobbies: white suits with blue trim and red kerchiefs. Two major-leaguers also awaited them: Eddie Ainsmith, who had caught Walter Johnson on the Washington Senators, and Earl Hamilton, who had pitched for the Pittsburgh Pirates. Although Ainsmith added sixteen-year-old Chicago pitcher Leona Kerns to the team, he and Hamilton would be the Bobbies' battery in Japan.

Former major-leaguer Ainsmith wasn't prepared for the fact that the Bobbies' shortstop was a kid. He must have worried whether he could launch a powerful throw down to second base when the player waiting there was a thirteen-year-old—how could she possibly catch it? So the catcher tried bribery, promising Edith a

Japanese yen for every time she caught a throw. Edith shrugged. "Sure," she said. Then, even though Ainsmith "could really fire them down," she commenced to catch everything that came her way. "I took him for plenty of yen," she laughs.

On October 18 the Bobbies arrived in Yokohama. Wearing long-waisted dresses or long sweaters over skirts, trench coats, cloche hats, opaque stockings, and heels, the young women posed with Japanese-inscribed banners and looked delighted to be there. They also looked far too young and inexperienced to win baseball games.

At first the "American Team," as they were called, was a tremendous attraction, drawing large crowds when playing against college teams and amateurs such as the Actors of Japan and the Movie Commentators (people who supplied the "comment" for silent movies). Edith drew long applause for her hitting and fielding, and the press, Japanese- and English-language alike, praised her unstintingly.

Bobbies in Japan: Eddie Ainsmith, left; Earl Hamilton, right; Edith Houghton, front center

But while Edith was a superior ballplayer, offensively and defensively, most of the Bobbies were not. The press and public soon tired of them—as did their sponsors, who failed to pay the game money or the fare back to the States. Ainsmith and O'Gara differed on how to proceed, and on November 13 Ainsmith and Hamilton and their wives, along with Leona Kerns, Edith Ruth, and Nellie Shank, left for Formosa (Taiwan), while O'Gara and the remaining Bobbies stayed in Kobe. A hotel owner eventually took pity on them and financed their passage to Seattle. They arrived back in Philadelphia on December 6, 1925.

Once back home, Edith Houghton and the Bobbies parted ways, with the Kid going on to play baseball for other teams. At one time or another in her career she played every position on the field, including pitcher and catcher. For a time, she played with the Passaic (N.J.) Bloomer Girls against Pennsylvania men's teams. "The performance of Edith Houghton for the invading team was the feature of the game," wrote one reporter. "This Miss played as good a brand of ball as any male player has displayed at Maple Shade this season. In addition to pasting out five hits, including two doubles and a screaming homer, she handled six tries at short in major league fashion."

Invited to play with Margaret Nabel and the New York Bloomer Girls for $35 a week, Edith accepted, commuting between Philadelphia and New York three times a week just to play baseball. Houghton's reputation grew along the East Coast, and when she was nineteen years old, she received a letter from a Boston promoter asking her to tour with his bloomer Hollywood Girls from April through October of 1931. The Kid was again paid $35 a week—good money during the Depression. Barnstorming through Texas and Oklahoma, the Hollywood Girls often played against minor league teams. Both Houghton and her former teammate Edith Ruth were on the roster of the Hollywood Girls, which, like the Bobbies, did not carry male players.

As the bloomer era drew to a close in 1933, the now tall and slender Kid, twenty-one years old, stuck close to home. She approached the Fisher A.A.'s, a men's semipro outfit. "I don't know what was in me," she says, "but I wasn't afraid to say, 'Will you give me a tryout?' I must have asked them, because I remember a tryout. They gave me a uniform and told me to play." Playing first base, Edith performed well for the Fisher A.A.'s. A reporter who interviewed her then wrote that "the men treat her just the same as though she legitimately belonged in trousers. They send the ball over the plate to her with just as much speed, and throw them to first base with as much zip as though she had a couple of baseball hams for hands."

Eventually young Houghton was faced with a choice she didn't want to make. By the mid 1930s, there were no more baseball opportunities for women. Because she wanted to stay active on the diamond, the Kid had no choice but to go where women were now confined—to softball. At first she disliked it, and she still insists indignantly that she did it only "because there was no baseball for women!" After a while she finally mastered the knack of hitting the large, heavy softball, and for several years she played with the Roverettes in Madison Square Garden.

After the United States entered World War II, Edith Houghton enlisted in the WAVES (Women Appointed for Volunteer

Emergency Service—U.S. Navy auxiliaries). While working in supplies and accounts, she tried out for the department's baseball team and was readily accepted. One Navy newsletter praised her by saying that "enlisted WAVE Houghton . . . can make any ball team in the country." Edith particularly enjoyed her Navy baseball days because the paucity of good pitching enabled her to hit .800 during a streak. Today she regrets that in the armed forces softball has replaced baseball. "I understand," she says reluctantly. "They didn't have the space or money for diamonds . . . and not everybody can play baseball."

After being discharged from the service, thirty-four-year-old Houghton landed a job as a glassware buyer for a Philadelphia wholesaler. But how could glass compare to diamonds? Early in 1946 she wrote to Bob Carpenter, owner of the last-place Philadelphia Phillies, and asked for an interview. Placing her baseball scrapbook on Carpenter's desk, Edith explained that she wanted a job as a scout for the Phillies. "He asked questions," she says. "I gave answers. I left the scrapbook with him." Several days later, Edith was called back. "Yeah," Carpenter said, "we'd like to have you." The Phillies' hiring of Houghton made national news, most of it very favorable. In Philadelphia, she scouted the sandlots and high schools, signing approximately fifteen players in six years. Two made it to Class B ball.

Edith Houghton was called up by the Navy in the early 1950s, during the Korean War. When she got out, she didn't return to scouting. "The way I feel about scouting is if you see somebody who's great, you can bet your buttons ten others are after him, too." Eventually she retired to Florida, where she's still drawn by

Houghton scouting for Philadelphia Phillies

the power of the diamond, attending the spring training games of the Phillies and the White Sox and watching baseball on television, particularly the Cubs and Phillies. Edith Houghton continues to live baseball.

"That slip of a girl, Edith Houghton—she's nearly 13 years old and stands nearly 5 feet in her nearly white kiddies' socks—almost won a game yesterday for the Bobbies from the Nippon Dental College baseball team. . . .

"She nominally played shortstop, but [was taking] all the throws to second and best of all pulling the famous Hans Wagner 'hidden ball' stunt that brought the crowd to their feet in admiration. . . .

"It came in the fourth inning. Masuda led off with a double to center and pulled up at second. Sara Conlin shot the ball to The Kid, and while Masuda was brushing off the dust and the coaches were looking down at their shoes and the boys on the bench cheering, little Miss Houghton slyly made a backhand toss to Chick Nolan who laid the ball away in her glove and went about her business. The Kid might have hidden the ball herself but she isn't much larger than the ball so she entrusted it to Miss Nolan.

"Then as Earl Hamilton turned toward home plate, and Masuda played off, The Kid stepped on the bag and Miss Nolan conjured the ball out of air for the little shortstop. The Kid promptly poked Masuda in the ribs and ran off kicking up her heels while Mr. Masuda looked painfully unnecessary and walked to the bench. Twice more during the rest of the game The Kid tried the same thing but by that time the eyes of Japan were on her so much that she couldn't have hidden a moth ball."

— *The Japan Advertiser,*
November 7, 1925

Margaret Gisolo

It all started in the small, closely knit community of Blanford, Indiana, where the men worked dangerous coal mines for little pay and the women made ends meet by gardening, canning, and making do. Here families surnamed Taparo, Semancik, Gisolo, Perona, and Marcenko believed that their children could and would take advantage of opportunities for a better life.

Born in Blanford on October 21, 1914, Margaret Gisolo was taught to play baseball by her oldest brother, Toney, a semipro and minor league player. Unlike her two older sisters, she took to the game immediately, pitching for her grade school team and playing sandlot games after class. When an unexpected baseball opportunity came Blanford's way in 1928, Margaret stepped in and took it.

That was the year the American Legion established a national baseball program for young people. Described by the *Indianapolis Times* as "a means of teaching practical Americanism to the youth of the country," American Legion Junior baseball got off to a solid start in 1928 and continues to this day. Recognizing the importance of junior baseball, the American and National leagues contributed $50,000 to the Junior World Series in 1928.

In Blanford, Margaret signed up for the newly created junior team, the Cubs, and was readily accepted. The Cubs and other junior teams played regular games until mid-June, when tournament play leading to the Junior World Series began.

On June 18 the Blanford Cubs faced the rival Clinton Baptists in a best-of-three series to determine the championship of Vermillion County. The teams were evenly matched, and the first game went into extra innings with the score tied, 7–7. The hit that won the game came from the bat of second baseman Margaret Gisolo, who in the top of the twelfth singled to short right to drive in the winning run.

After Blanford's triumph, Clinton officials protested the game because a girl had played. Quoting American Legion regulations that "any boy was eligible to play" who met the age requirements, they argued that by inference no girl was eligible to play. Such a shameless attempt to snatch an unearned victory caused the *Indianapolis Times* to chide Clinton for its poor sportsmanship.

While officials pondered the protest, tournament play continued. In the second game of the Blanford-Clinton match, on June 24, the Cubs defeated the Baptists a second time, and Blanford was jubilant. But then Robert Bushee, Indiana American Legion state athletic officer, stepped in to suspend Gisolo for six days. During that time, Bushee met with state director Dan Sowers, who met with Baseball Commissioner Kenesaw Mountain Landis, all over the question of an outstanding player who was causing an uproar simply because she was female. Ultimately, the three men ruled that Margaret was eligible to play because "while the National Junior baseball program of the American Legion did

"Apparently it was [okay] with Clinton for Margaret to play second base for the opposition until she got too good."

—*The Indianapolis Times,*
June 27, 1928

COMPARABLE OR BETTER

"It points out the real discrimination in society. Margaret Gisolo was a second baseperson comparable to or better than any others around her. She had a sense of doing the right thing at the right time and was the person of the hour. What happened demonstrates that despite her gift, society's bias level dictates different positions for different people. This hasn't changed much in all the years."

—Tony Ladd, Chairman of the Department of Physical Education, Wheaton College, and author of a paper on Margaret Gisolo, commenting on the ruling against girls in American Legion Junior Baseball

not contemplate the participation of girls there was nothing specifically stated in the rules which would bar them from playing on competing teams."

Having ruled that Gisolo could play, Bushee then forfeited the first Blanford victory to Clinton—not because a girl had played, but because Gambiana, one of the other Blanford players, was over the age limit of seventeen. Meanwhile Margaret, only vaguely aware of the controversy surrounding her, simply continued playing baseball. In the deciding game, the Cubs turned back the Baptists, 5–2.

"It was an unusually good team," says Gisolo. "We worked so well together. There was a feeling of cooperation." Margaret regularly stole bases, drove in runs, turned double plays, and fielded her position flawlessly. The eyes of the state and the nation upon them, the young team from the coal-mining town was poised to move up the tournament ladder.

On July 6 the Cubs faced the Terre Haute Blue Devils in a one-game playoff. When the game had ended, the *Terre Haute Spectator* philosophized that "the sand lots and the commons where all the real ball players come from had their innings at the stadium Wednesday afternoon." Aided by a Gisolo hit that drove in two runs, the Cubs defeated the Blue Devils, 6–5. Around this time, Margaret received a present from Commissioner Landis: a baseball that he had autographed "To Margaret Gisolo, With my very good wishes."

The next step up the tournament ladder for the "kids from the mining camp" was a game against the big-city Evansville West Side Nuts on July 24. With little effort, the Cubs shelled their opponents, 26–7, with Margaret "accepting six chances at second and scoring several of her team's runs." Two days later, Blanford faced the highly favored Gary Yanks at Indianapolis's Riverside Park. At stake was the state championship.

The Cubs came out swinging, pounding out six runs in the top of the first. "We ain't had our bats," a Gary player informed them, and in the bottom of the first the Yanks thumped the Cubs for eight runs. The lead then seesawed back and forth, the Cubs' runs coming from the stick work of Sungali, Taparo, and Gisolo. In the top of the sixth, the Cubs took a one-run lead and proceeded to shut down the Yanks' hitting. After pushing an insurance run across the plate in the final inning, Blanford won the Indiana American Legion Junior championship by a score of 14–12. In seven games of tournament play, Margaret Gisolo had pounded out nine hits in twenty-one at-bats (.429) and made ten putouts and twenty-eight assists with no errors. Across the nation, girls who loved baseball tried to sign up for American Legion Junior teams.

Toney and Margaret Gisolo, 1928

On August 9, in the large and imposing Comiskey Park, Blanford faced the Chicago Marine Post team in the Indiana-Illinois playoff. Margaret remembers what a thrill it was for her to hear the loudspeaker announcement: "Gisolo up to bat!" But the thrill of victory did not come to the Cubs, who lost the first round of interstate play by a score of 12–5.

The Cubs were welcomed back to Blanford as heroes. At an end-of-season banquet given by the American Legion, the boys received watch fobs and Margaret was given a gold-plated pin— a miniature baseball mitt holding a white ball.

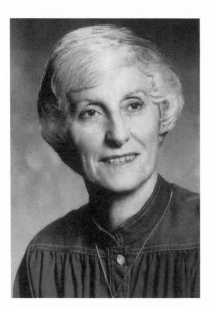

Margaret Gisolo, Chairperson Emeritus, Department of Dance, Arizona State University

Then something completely unexpected happened: Margaret Gisolo was told that the American Legion had written a new rule to exclude girls from Junior baseball. She could no longer play for the Cubs. Her teammates and the townspeople were stunned. "Everyone at the banquet was asking why," she remembers. The Legion's answer was that if girls played, they would need separate dressing rooms, separate hotel rooms, and chaperones. Nobody from Blanford wanted this rule, but there it stood until the 1970s, when girls were allowed back into American Legion Junior baseball.

Officially excluded from playing with her lifelong teammates, Margaret Gisolo still got to play the game she loved—thanks to her own talent and to the indefatigable Maud Nelson, who was fielding a bloomer team named the All Star Ranger Girls. Early in 1929, Nelson wrote to Toney Gisolo to arrange a tryout for him and Margaret. After a brief stint with Rose Figg's American Athletic Girls (a team started by Maud Nelson in 1914), Margaret played with the Ranger Girls during the summers of 1930 through 1934. (For part of 1931, she also played with the Hollywood Movie Stars Baseball Team.) Both the opportunity to play baseball and the money earned were important to Gisolo. The opportunity to play confirmed her growing self-confidence, and the money enabled her to attend college.

Between 1935 and 1954, Margaret Gisolo had a wide and varied career, similar to that of Amanda Clement. Among other things, she was supervisor of physical education for the public school system of Paris, Indiana; attended the University of California and New York University; joined the WAVES, entering the

U.S. Navy as an ensign and leaving as a lieutenant commander; and taught physical education at the college level.

In 1954 she was hired by Arizona State University as an instructor of tennis and dance in women's physical education. There she stayed, in a new community that would accept and respect her as warmly as had Blanford. Through her work, creativity, and vision for the future, ASU moved from offering dance as part of physical education to developing a nationally recognized Department of Dance. Upon her retirement in 1980, *Arizona Arts and Lifestyle Magazine* wrote that "for Arizonans, the cultural climate of an entire state has changed with the help of one person—Margaret Gisolo."

After retiring, Margaret concentrated on her tennis and in both 1989 and 1991 she and her partner won gold medals in doubles tennis at the Senior Olympics. A creative, intelligent woman with a clever sense of humor, Margaret Gisolo dwells on the positive aspects of her ballplaying days. "I'm amazed at the results of my playing," she says, counting her whole exciting life as part of the results. "The sense of achievement and accomplishment was very positive, and that has stayed with me."

"The party of the first part, Rose Figg, hereby agrees to pay Margaret Gisolo, or her mother, Seventy Five Dollars per month, for the services of Margaret Gisolo as ball player for the season of 1929, together with room, board and transportation, and to return her to her home when the season closes.

"Season begins about the Middle of May.

"The party of the first part, Rose Figg, will furnish a complete base ball uniform, and Margaret Gisolo shall furnish her own base ball bat, shoes, glove and sweater."

—from the contract between Margaret Gisolo and Rose Figg's American Athletic Girls

Jackie Mitchell

"She uses an odd, side-armed delivery, and puts both speed and curve on the ball. Her greatest asset, however, is control. She can place the ball where she pleases, and her knack at guessing the weakness of a batter is uncanny. . . .

"She doesn't hope to enter the big show this season, but she believes that with careful training she may soon be the first woman to pitch in the big leagues. In that event she sees no reason why she shouldn't command as great a salary as Babe Ruth now draws."

—*The Chattanooga News,*
March 31, 1931

IN THE COLD, WET SPRING OF 1931, YOUNG VIRNE BEATRICE "Jackie" Mitchell became the second woman ever signed to a minor league contract. Reporters at the time, not knowing about Lizzie Arlington, hailed the signing as a first. Much news that once would have remained local, as did Arlington's story in 1898, now reached a national audience through radio. The story of a young woman overcoming barriers excited people trapped in the midst of the Great Depression.

The story began in Chattanooga, with a Class AA minor league team owned by Joe Engel, a former pitcher for the Washington Senators. A man who loved promotions and publicity, Engel filled the ballpark on one occasion by raffling off a house; on another, by staging an elephant hunt. In March 1931, Joe Engel signed Jackie Mitchell to a minor league contract with the Chattanooga Lookouts; her father, Dr. Joe Mitchell, acted as her agent.

Local papers immediately picked up the story, and at first Jackie confessed, "To tell the truth, all I want is to stay in professional baseball long enough to get money to buy a roadster." Later, she amended that statement: "I hope to pitch for years to come and shall try to get into a World Series." As soon as Engel announced that the rookie southpaw would pitch in an exhibition game against the New York Yankees, who were making their way north from spring training, other papers picked up the story. Only the conservative *Sporting News* refused to carry it, wiring back to a local reporter: "Quit your kidding. What is Chattanooga trying to do? Burlesque the game?"

But Jackie Mitchell was the real thing. At age seventeen, she stood five feet, seven inches tall and weighed 130 pounds. She had not always been so robust: a premature baby, she had weighed four pounds at birth. Because the family doctor had advised her parents to give her fresh air and exercise, she grew up athletic. "I was out at the sandlots with father from as long as I can remember," she once explained. When she was seven or eight years old, Dazzy Vance, star pitcher for the Brooklyn Dodgers, taught her how to pitch.

As a teenager, Jackie played baseball in Chattanooga and in one amateur game struck out nine men. In March 1931 she attended Norman "Kid" Elberfeld's baseball camp in Atlanta, the only baseball school of its kind at the time, frequented by beginners as well as by major-leaguers such as Luke Appling.

"I don't know what's going to happen if they begin to let women in baseball. Of course, they will never make good. Why? Because they are too delicate. It would kill them to play ball every day."

—Babe Ruth

Pregame activity: Lou Gehrig, Babe Ruth, Jackie Mitchell

"[The Yankees] will meet a club here that has a girl pitcher named Jackie Mitchell, who has a swell change of pace and swings a mean lipstick.

"I suppose that in the next town the Yankees enter they will find a squad that has a female impersonator in left field, a sword swallower at short and a trained seal behind the plate. Times in the South are not only tough but silly."

—*The New York Daily News,*
April 2, 1931

Revealing all these details in countless stories, reporters dug for more. Dr. Joseph Mitchell told them that his daughter was "a curve-ball pitcher, not a smoke-ball pitcher," but he assured them she could do the job against the Yankees. When Babe Ruth was interviewed, he shook his head in bewilderment. "By the way," he asked reporters, "how big is she?" When told Jackie's height and weight, the Sultan of Swat muttered, "Well, I don't know what things are coming to."

The Yankees-Lookouts game was scheduled for April 1, but a downpour soaked the field and pushed the game to April 2. On that cloudy and cool Thursday, both teams took pregame practice at Engel Stadium (a mere three blocks from Jackie's home) while a crowd of four thousand flooded through the turnstiles and filled every available seat. With scores of reporters, wire services, and even a film crew from Universal Newsreel on hand, the game began.

Manager Bert Niehoff sent Clyde Barfoot to the mound against the Yankees. The Lookout pitcher immediately gave up a double and a single: after the first two batters, the score stood at 1–0. Niehoff then strode to the hill, yanked his starter, and put in Jackie Mitchell to face Babe Ruth.

Clad in a baggy white uniform specially sewn for her by Spalding Company, a large *C* visible on her cap, Mitchell took a few warmup pitches before Ruth, batting third, stepped into the batter's box. A southpaw, Jackie had only one pitch—"a mean drop pitch." Ruth took ball one, then swung at the next two pitches and missed. Jackie's fourth pitch was a called strike. The Babe, possibly hamming it up, "kicked the dirt, called the umpire a few dirty names, gave his bat a wild heave and stomped off to the Yanks' dugout." The *Chattanooga News* reported that "Mr. Ruth . . . acted in a rude manner which would never have done for the Lees and the Randolphs of the old South."

Lou Gehrig then came to the plate. Mitchell threw him three pitches and he swung at each, connecting with nothing but Chattanooga mountaintop air. Seventeen-year-old Jackie Mitchell had just fanned Babe Ruth and Lou Gehrig back-to-back. Grinning and shaking his head, Gehrig larruped back to the dugout while Tony Lazzeri, who had been watching from the on-deck circle with every intention of hitting the rookie pitcher, stepped to the plate. Lazzeri swung at Mitchell's first pitch, fouling it off. He took the next four and drew a base on balls. At this point Niehoff marched to the mound again, pulling Mitchell and reinstating Barfoot. The Yankees won, 14–4.

Years later, Jackie Mitchell recalled that after she struck out Gehrig, it "set off a standing ovation . . . that must have lasted ten minutes." Most likely she was exaggerating. But the amount of fan mail she received after the feat was staggering. From around the nation people took her side. So much mail came addressed to "The Girl Who Struck Out Ruth and Gehrig, Chattanooga, Tennessee," that the post office delivered it in bulk mail bags. "I had so much mail coming in, my daddy had to hire a secretary to answer it all," she remembered.

On the day the Yankees fanned, the debate began: Was it real, or was it a stunt? The world would never know, for Commissioner Kenesaw Mountain Landis stepped in, voiding Jackie's contract on the grounds that life in baseball was "too strenuous" for a woman.

"Cynics may contend that on the diamond as elsewhere it is *place aux dames*. Perhaps Miss Jackie hasn't quite enough on the ball yet to bewilder Ruth and Gehrig in a serious game. But there are no such sluggers in the Southern Association, and she may win laurels this season which cannot be ascribed to mere gallantry. The prospect grows gloomier for misogynists."

—*The New York Times*, April 4, 1931

Jackie was crushed. Ice-cold water had been poured over her dreams of material wealth (the roadster) and glory (the World Series). Nobody prominent protested or came to her defense: not Joe Engel, not Dr. Mitchell, not the media. In those days, the rulings of baseball's czar were absolute.

The czar, however, ruled only the major and minor leagues. Within a month of Landis's ruling, Jackie Mitchell was back in baseball as the star attraction of a hastily improvised team called the Junior Lookouts (sometimes dubbed the Lookout Juniors). Managed by ex-major-leaguer Kid Elberfeld, the Juniors fielded had-been and would-be minor leaguers. Elberfeld easily booked games throughout eastern Tennessee as town and semipro teams accepted the challenge from Jackie and the Juniors.

With Jackie pitching the first two or three innings of each game, the Juniors were quite successful, winning five out of six games on one trip, twelve out of sixteen on another. Win or lose, however, the principal draw was the young woman pitcher. She even returned to Chattanooga where, at the end of May, she and the Lookout Juniors faced Margaret Nabel and the New York Bloomer Girls. Like the game against the Yankees, this one was also a sellout. And the four thousand fans who packed the stadium weren't disappointed. Pitching three innings, the young local held the "Yorkers" hitless, and the Juniors defeated the Bloomers, 7–4.

By July 1931, Jackie Mitchell had so many offers to pitch in exhibition games that she left the Juniors and headed north. Her first stop was Cleveland, Ohio, where she pitched under arc lights. Throughout 1932 she continued to tour, traveling with her father and mother and pitching at exhibition games. Then, in 1933, the *New York Times* reported that nineteen-year-old Jackie Mitchell was signed to "occupy the pitcher's mound [with the] bearded and long-locked House of David" and that she would receive $1,000 a month through the rest of the season. House of David teams, originating out of Benton Harbor, Michigan, had been barnstorming since the turn of the century and were known to baseball fans everywhere.

A life of banishment from baseball's best circuits was hard on Mitchell. There was nowhere for her to go but sideways. From 1933 through 1937 she traveled with the House, pitching an inning or two every day. While taking on local teams must have been fun, there was a silly and demeaning side to some of the promotions—playing baseball while riding donkeys, for example. After seven years, Jackie tired of it and returned to Chattanooga, where she worked in her father's office. When she was in her fifties she married Eugene Gilbert, a man she had known most of her life. To her neighbors, she was known simply as Jackie Gilbert and few, if any, remembered her story.

Not even Alan Morris, sports editor of the *Chattanooga News-Free Press*, knew what had happened to Jackie Mitchell when in 1975 he received a letter from California asking, "Whatever happened to the girl who struck out Babe Ruth?" When Jackie saw Morris's column, she called him up. Her story was retold and suddenly a new generation was interested. Once again, she received congratulatory letters by the hundreds, letters from average people who, amazed and impressed, wanted the Jackies of the world to win.

Mitchell, probably while touring with House of David

To the satisfaction of her fans, Mitchell proved as feisty and controversial as ever. "I'm interested in keeping up with what's happening in female athletics and efforts of the girls to play against the boys," she told reporters. "There is one woman umpire in professional baseball now and maybe some day there will be a player in the big leagues."

Jackie Mitchell died in 1987, at the age of seventy-three.

IN PERSPECTIVE

David Jenkins, sports reporter for the *Chattanooga News-Free Press*, got to know Jackie Mitchell in the last few years of her life, even traveling with her to her first major league baseball game in Atlanta. He saw the film of her striking out Ruth and Gehrig and feels that it "isn't really conclusive." But, he says, "She threw well enough to have the ball do things. It was a drop ball, a sinker. She [knew] what to do with it. The players may have gone along with the thing in good fun, but that doesn't mean they weren't struck out. She might have been doing more than they expected her to do."

Mitchell was the kind of person, says Jenkins, who had strong opinions and feelings. "For Engel, it was just a promotion, that's all. It could have been real or not, but it was just a promotion. For Jackie it was very real. She had a very active mind. Women's rights appealed to her. She was victimized by Landis. She had wanted a career in athletics.

"If Engel had backed Jackie in trying to assert her right to play baseball—in asserting the validity of the contract—she would probably have gone ahead and fought against the rescinding of the contract. But nobody backed her."

To Jenkins, the woman who struck out Ruth and Gehrig represented the possibility of better things. "Her pioneer spirit was her greatest achievement," he concludes. "Jackie didn't care what people thought. She was truly a peer of Babe Didrikson, Helen Wills, and other great women athletes of the time."

Babe Didrikson

MILDRED ELLA DIDRIKSON, KNOWN TO THE WORLD AS BABE, was a braggart. "I came out to beat everybody in sight and that's just what I'm going to do," she shouted to reporters at the 1932 Los Angeles Olympics. Babe bragged so often and so stingingly that her Olympic teammates detested her. Jean Shiley, who competed against Babe in the high jump, recalled that no matter what another teammate said she had done, Didrikson would interrupt with, "Oh, I done that and I done it in *half* the time."

An extraordinary athlete, Didrikson mastered any sport she attempted, from rough-and-tumble basketball to silent-concentration golf. Two years after she graduated from Beaumont (Tex.) High School, Babe made national news when she entered the Amateur Athletic Union championships and out of eight events, won five, tied one, and finished fourth in another, thus single-handedly winning the *team* title for track and field. Permitted to enter only three events at the Olympics, she won two gold medals and one silver; although her high jump tied Jean Shiley's, the judges awarded Babe the silver because they disapproved of her unorthodox style.

A baseball player from her earliest days, young Mildred

"A woman's place is in or around the home. I was glad to give this dame a lift, but there's such a thing as carrying a thing too far."

—Frankie Frisch, Cardinals' manager, upon yanking Babe Didrikson after she gave up three runs to the Red Sox in the first inning

Years after Babe left baseball and become a golf champion, she tried to enter the baseball players' links tourney in Miami. Didrikson explained that she was entitled to play golf in the tournament because she had signed a contract with the St. Louis Cardinals in 1934 for an exhibition game and had never been released. Her request was turned down.

Didrikson slugged the ball so hard and so far that her teammates tagged her Babe, after Babe Ruth. The nickname stuck like pine tar: even her parents called her Babe. At an AAU meet, she picked up a baseball and hurled it 296 feet—a world record for women. Yet when it came to the national pastime, the great braggart was reticent. Baseball didn't bring the Babe to her knees, exactly, but it did humble her.

Although Didrikson yearned to turn professional after the Olympics, there were few sports in which women could earn money, so when promoter Ray Doan offered her $1,000 a month to tour with a men's basketball team to be called Babe Didrikson's All-Americans, she accepted. Louis "Boze" Berger, who would go on to play second base for the Cleveland Indians, remembers that his college basketball team played against the All-Americans in 1934. "We won," he says, "but she was all over you."

At the end of the basketball season, Babe agreed to appear with Doan's House of David baseball team, again for $1,000 a month. Waiting for the House to begin barnstorming, she went south, where the "grapefruit circuit" teams held spring training. There she pitched exhibition games against both major and minor league teams. Against the latter, she fared well.

In New Orleans, the Babe won high praise when she took the mound for the Cleveland Indians against their minor league club, the Pelicans. Roy Hughes, who would be called up by Cleveland next year, played for the Pelicans on that day in 1934 and remembers that it was tough to get a hit off Didrikson. She hurled two scoreless innings and batted twice, earning praise from everyone.

Pitching against major-leaguers was another story. In Fort Myers,

Florida, Didrikson appeared for the Philadelphia Athletics against the Brooklyn Dodgers, walking one batter and hitting another, but getting out of the inning safely when the Dodgers hit into a triple play.

Although she lucked out against the Dodgers, Babe was pounded by both the Red Sox and the Athletics. In Bradenton, Cardinals' manager Frankie Frisch yanked her in the first inning after she gave up three runs to the Red Sox. Taking the mound against the Athletics in another game, she loaded the bases with no outs. "Those bases got loaded on hits, not walks," she later said. "I always had pretty good control. I seldom walked anybody. But I couldn't seem to throw the ball past these major-leaguers." The next batter hit into a double play and nobody scored. Then "Double X," slugger Jimmie Foxx, came to bat.

Babe Didrikson on mound for Cleveland Indians, New Orleans, 1934

"I pitched to Jimmie Foxx and gave him my high, hard one," she explained. "Foxx knocked it into the next county." Actually, he knocked it into one of the orange trees that served as the outfield "fence." Chasing it, Paul Dean disappeared into the grove and returned with five oranges in his glove. With very little to brag about, Didrikson actually wondered if the major leaguers were laughing at her. "Jimmie Foxx may have been thinking, 'Go home, girl, and jerk sodas, . . .'" she admitted. "But he was considerate."

Spring training behind her, Babe barnstormed with the House of David from Florida to Idaho, pitching at least one inning in approximately two hundred games. But pitching was not the Babe's greatest strength. Ironically, baseball humbled her because it wouldn't make use of her best abilities—running and hitting.

Organized baseball thought of Didrikson (as well as of Arlington and Mitchell) as a specialized player (pitcher), not as an all-round baseball player able to hit, field, and run.

Running the 80-yard dash faster than many major-leaguers, the Babe could have been a terror on the basepaths. Sports reporters who were impressed with her pitching were at least equally impressed with her hitting and running. Ed McAuley of the *Cleveland News* wrote, "Miss Didrikson then proceeded to show real power in her batting swing. She sent a whistling foul down the left field line, a fly to right and—in her second time at bat—a sharp single to left." For the *Cleveland Press*, Stuart Bell opined, "The Babe stood up to the plate without flinching and took a man-sized cut. . . . The next time she came to bat she walloped a clean line drive over the New Orleans shortstop's head for a single, raced down to first base with all the speed that made her a sensation at the last Olympic games, turned the bag in approved style and dashed back as the throw came in from the outfield." Emphasizing that "the Babe takes that bat off her shoulder and swings it," Bell suggested that Cleveland officials sign her.

Others concurred. House of David player Emory Olive felt that Didrikson "wasn't really all that good a pitcher," but vouched that "she could hit pretty good. Once at Logan Park in Chicago we were playing before eight thousand people and she hit a long line drive that she turned into a homer: it was the only run scored in the game."

In the tightly controlled and protected world of organized baseball, it didn't matter how well Babe Didrikson could hit, run, or field. Or pitch, for that matter. Commissioner Kenesaw Mountain

Landis, who had voided Jackie Mitchell's contract three years earlier, would never have allowed her to enter the game. The Babe knew this, and so, when the 1934 season was over, she went on to earn an athletic living in a different sport, dominating women's golf until her death in 1956.

Didrikson in Yankee Stadium, 1948

"The House of David baseball club has signed Babe Didrikson, the world's greatest woman athlete, to pitch for them. She draws the largest salary of any independent baseball player in the country. She has played baseball since childhood with her brothers and their companions, and if she had devoted all her athletic efforts to baseball like most major league players have in their youth, no doubt she would have been a major league pitcher. She pitches a part of every game the House of David plays and takes her regular turn at bat. She asks no favor and gives none to her masculine opponents. The Babe pitches just like a man. She can throw a fast ball and works a change of pace, mixed with a fast breaking curve ball.

"The fans get their greatest thrill when Miss Didrikson strikes out her opponents. The Babe says she really gets a kick out of it too. The Babe is easily spotted on the diamond before the game among the twenty-five or more ball players working out, as there are very few ball players as fast as Miss Didrikson. The fans will not only see Babe pitch, but they will see her go through all the warming up exercises that the other ball players do before the game."

—*Altoona Mirror,*
August 14, 1934

The All Star Ranger Girls

As co-owner and manager of the All Star Ranger Girls, Maud Nelson passed her knowledge and skills on to a third generation of young women and men. When there was no longer a place for barnstorming women, she retired—but not before providing the living link between the heroic history of bloomer baseball and the magnificent league that was to come.

With the Rangers, Nelson employed most of the same tactics she had earlier used with the Western Bloomer Girls. She once again preferred co-owning a team, this time with her second husband, Costante Dellacqua, as her partner. And she continued to devise imaginative ways to get the attention of potential fans: hiring a band to lead the team and townspeople to the ballpark remained a favorite. With the All Star Ranger Girls, Maud also used flashy uniforms to get the attention of the reporters, photographers, and fans. On the field, the Rangers wore plain flannel uniforms. Off the field, they were the most showily dressed of Nelson's players, sporting cowboy hats, silky jackets, and flared skirts modeled after the Hollywood cowboy look. The fans remembered the distinct apparel and the players savored it. "I loved those cowboy hats and dark jackets," says Rose Gacioch. "Those were made for me."

The All Star Ranger Girls and Costante Dellacqua

Like all of Maud's teams, the Rangers were composed of good baseball players whom she recruited from as broad a geographical base as possible. In 1927 a car accident sent two of her female players back to Chicago for recuperation. Nelson simply looked around Westmoreland County, Pennsylvania, where the Rangers were playing, and, using her many connections, recruited young Alice Lopes and Margaret Watson. A few weeks later Lopes was pitching in Adrian, Michigan, where the local paper reported: "Miss Lopes hurled for the first five innings and demonstrated that there was something more behind the ball than a mere pair of blue eyes and a boyish bob. A slow drop had the Adrian batters fooled for the first two innings and a still slower straight ball over the inside corner kept them fooled during the remainder of her turn on the rubber." In 1934, Maud Nelson made a special point of swinging the team through Wheeling, West Virginia, to give young Rose Gacioch a tryout. Liking what she saw, she added Gacioch to the team.

By 1930 the All Star Ranger Girls were a crackerjack team. Notable among the regulars were Beatrice "Peanuts" Schmidt, a heavy-hitting pitcher and second baseman from Kenosha, Wisconsin, and Elizabeth "Fargo" Pull of North Dakota, the team captain. Young Margaret Gisolo played first base like a major-leaguer. In center field, Tex Wines made spectacular, one-hand catches of long fly balls; later, Cecil "Montana" Gridle (or Griedel) would play this position. Although the Rangers did have some very bad days—they lost to the minor league Greensburg (Pa.) Generals, 14–1, in 1927 and to the Martinsburg (W. Va.) Blue Sox,

16–1, in 1934—they generally amassed tributes, particularly for the playing of Schmidt, Gisolo, and Gacioch.

Fielding three male players was also a Nelson tradition, one that she refined with the Rangers by devising a lineup in which every third batter was a man. The theory was that the women would get on base with singles, and the men—particularly Lee Chandler—would drive in the runs with extra-base hits.

Of all the Ranger teams, the one of 1934 may have been the best. Starting off in Illinois, they defeated the Mattoon nine, 11–8. In Athens, Ohio, they lost to the Eagles, 2–0, but, as a reporter praised, "looked the part" of a ball team. In New York they lost to a Schenectady team, 4–3, with pitchers Gacioch and Schmidt racking up six strikeouts and no walks. Gisolo played first base and batted cleanup. In Rhode Island the Rangers defeated a star men's team, 2–1, after Gacioch relayed the ball from the outfield to the shortstop, who snapped it to the plate in time to cut off the tying run. On the East Coast, so many teams wanted to play against the All Star Rangers that year that Margaret Gisolo remembers a few days on which the team played *three* different ball games.

But 1934 was the last year for the All Star Ranger Girls. Across the nation, bloomer teams were turning off the lights. The Western Bloomer Girls were gone, as were the American Athletic Girls and Margaret Nabel and the New York Bloomer Girls. Baseball for women was being replaced by softball. Corporations that formerly sponsored women's baseball now switched to less-expensive softball teams—teams that relied mainly on one outstanding player, the pitcher.

Rose Gacioch remembers the thrill of traveling with the Ranger Girls as an eighteen-year-old rookie. For the first time, she visited New England and toured the Beechnut Chewing Gum factory, where each of the Rangers received free gum, manufactured in large squares. Later that day, Rose tucked some of the squares into the back pocket of her baseball uniform.

Playing the outfield, Gacioch felt the urge to chew. Just as she thrust her hand into her back pocket to take out the gum, the batter smashed a long line drive—and the ball whistled over Rose's head while her hand was still in her pocket. For that misdemeanor she was fined $50—a whole month's pay.

Toward the end of the season, the team headed home. When they reached Cleveland, Rose became homesick. "I wanted to go home, I didn't want to go on to Chicago," she says. "So they put me on a bus from Cleveland to Wheeling." And, to her surprise, the team captain returned her $50.

Maud's stepson Joe Dellacqua, who had traveled with the Ranger Girls, driving ahead of the team with Maud so she could book games, was getting married. Fargo Pull had reached the age of baseball retirement. Margaret Gisolo went on to a career teaching college. An era was ending.

Women would play baseball again. From 1943 to 1954 they played on the most professional, most highly paid women's teams the country has ever seen. But these teams were owned and controlled by men who required women to play the game with shorter basepaths and a larger, softer ball—concessions to women's supposed inferior abilities. A reduced perspective was never the tradition of bloomer teams, who faced their fellow athletes on equal terms.

In February of 1944, Maud Nelson died of heart failure. Two months later, Rose Gacioch was signed to play in the All-American Girls Baseball League. Gacioch went on to an eleven-year career: the link between the barnstorming bloomers and the women who—finally—played on fields of their own.

Part 3

THE

LEAGUE

YEARS

WHEN PHILIP K. WRIGLEY FOUNDED WHAT BECAME THE
All-American Girls Baseball League, his aim was not to restore
the game of baseball to women, but to entertain fans during a time
when many major-leaguers were off to war. This is not to say that
Wrigley was unsympathetic to women in sports—he simply
believed women could not play baseball. He therefore formed the
All-American Girls Softball League in 1943.

During its twelve-year existence, the league went through many
changes—in name, in the game itself, in organizational structure,
in managers, in location, and in players. The year after its found-
ing, it was called the All-American Girls Ball League, then the
All-American Girls Base Ball League, then the All-American
Girls Professional Base Ball League, then the American Girls
Baseball League. Most people today refer to it as the AAGBL or
the AAGPBL.

Changes in the game began from the moment of inception.
Although Wrigley called his group a softball league, the game
deviated from regulation softball in one important respect: stealing was permitted. The distances to the pitcher's mound and
between the bases were slightly longer than in softball, but it was
the first difference that was fundamental and pointed the way
toward baseball. In softball the pitcher is dominant, shutouts are
common, and batters go down in quick order. World-renowned
softball pitcher Joan Joyce said it best: "I'm boring to watch." By
permitting stealing, the men who ran the AAGBL began to take
the game away from the pitcher and give it to the runner.
Throughout league history, base-stealing was an exciting feature
of the games, and double steals weren't uncommon.

Part of the reason for the evolution of the AAGBL game from softball to baseball was that the team managers were, by and large, former major-leaguers who loved the complexities and challenge of baseball. These men—particularly Max Carey, Hall of Fame outfielder and record-holding base-stealer—pushed the AAGBL game toward baseball, teaching the players the finer points of the national pastime. Then, too, the players themselves were such exceptional athletes that the men who managed them came to believe there was nothing these women couldn't do. Finally, league management, always concerned with what the public wanted, concluded that what fans liked most of all was a live ball—one that traveled fast and far and resonated with a resounding crack when the bat met it squarely. Thus the AAGBL ball slowly decreased in size from a twelve-inch softball to a 91/4-inch baseball. It can be said that all changes in the AAGBL flowed from those in the size of the ball, for the smaller, harder, and more lively the ball became, the farther back the mound had to be moved and the farther apart the basepaths had to be set.

During its twelve-year history, the AAGBL went through three organizational phases: Wrigley ownership and management (1943–44); management under Arthur Meyerhoff through the League Board (1945–50); and management in which local teams went their own way (1951–54). Wrigley put up the money to start the first four teams and paid for the advertising. Meyerhoff, who ran the advertising agency Wrigley used, bought the league from the chewing-gum magnate and ran it in a similar fashion. Meyerhoff's management included systematic publicity for the AAGBL and required each franchise to turn part of its gate money over to the central organizational structure, to be used for publicity and promotions of various kinds.

Although Meyerhoff's superior understanding guided the league through its most profitable days, he made one mistake that caused everlasting dissension within the board of directors: in 1948 he expanded the AAGBL to ten teams, a move that many felt diluted the talent and caliber of play and that within one month resulted in the financial failure of the two new teams. The Chicago Colleens and the Springfield Sallies were thus carried by gate proceeds from the other eight teams for the rest of the year, amid much grumbling and dissension among the solvent franchises.

At the end of the 1950 season, the franchise owners bought Meyerhoff out and entered the period of independent management. Cutting back on spring training and on publicity and promotion in a time when league attendance was dwindling, the board of directors found themselves running out of players, fans, and viable franchises all at once. The AAGBL played its last game in September 1954.

Although the league played only in the Midwest, it drew players from more than half of the forty-eight states, from Canada, and from Cuba. In all, close to six hundred women played professional baseball in the All-American Girls Baseball League. Promoting its players as good-looking, feminine, "All-American" women who were teachers, secretaries, models, clerks, and the like, the league paid them very well. The overwhelming majority of players were from the working-class—athletic young women who loved the diamond game and jumped at the chance to earn $45–$75 a week, an amount four times what they could make at jobs traditionally reserved for women. Many sent money home to their families. Most were single, a few were married, a few were mothers.

In forming the AAGBL, Wrigley imposed on the players his beliefs (and those of society as a whole) that sport was a masculine exercise, not a gender-neutral one, and that women who were great athletes had to counterbalance their participation in a "masculine" endeavor by intensifying the kind of deportment that society considered feminine. Thus Wrigley made the female baseball players attend charm school and learn how to apply and wear makeup, how to sit, how to walk, how to stand, how to say "Ohhh" with rounded lips. On the field, ballplayers had to wear makeup at all times, were required to have long hair, and were sent onto the baseball diamond wearing one-piece dresses. At first the skirts were so long that they interfered with underhand pitching as well as with reaching down to scoop up grounders. Later the dresses were shortened, and when fans were purple with cold in the stands, huddling under blankets and sipping coffee from thermoses, the ballplayers had to take the field with bare thighs. When a player slid into base—and everyone was expected to steal bases—she bruised or abraded her skin on the hard ground of high school fields, many of them full of cinders and some burned over with gasoline and oil in order to make them dry enough to play on. Attended to in the dugout between innings, she then went out and did it again. And again and again.

League players put up with it all, some begrudgingly, some with humor, some unquestioningly, because only by doing so could they play baseball for a living.

For these few hundred fortunate women, playing baseball instilled courage and confidence beyond measure, so that when the game was over a large number of them went on to become doctors, lawyers, teachers—professions beyond their means and expectations before their baseball careers. It gave them camaraderie beyond average friendships; to this day, many rely on one another for support.

For those who actually saw them play, the women of the AAGBL changed forever the unquestioned concept that women cannot play baseball. For their managers, they played the national pastime as only professionals can. The ballplayers of the AAGBL were greater than the forces that produced them. They were equal to the game, as Max Carey believed, more serious than the skirts they were required to wear, more intelligent than the various board directors who would not let them become managers. At the end of the 1952 season, Jimmie Foxx, manager of the Fort Wayne Daisies, summed it up when he told his players: "You are true major leaguers in my eyes."

THE ROAD TO BASEBALL

The game of baseball started with underhand pitching and a shorter distance from
the mound to the plate than is used
today. Except for the size of the ball,
which has remained approximately the
same, baseball evolved into its present-
day sizes and dimensions over a period
of nearly fifty years.

The game played by the All-American
Girls Baseball League followed a similar
evolution, but completed it in twelve
years, as shown by the chart at right.
Occasionally league changes were introduced in mid-season; all sizes and
distances indicate those used in the
second half of the season.

	Ball	Mound	Basepaths	Pitching Delivery
1943	12″	40′	65′	underhand
1944	11½″	40′	68′	underhand
1945	11½″	42′	68′	underhand
1946	11″	43′	72′	underhand & sidearm
1947	11″	43′	72′	sidearm
1948	10⅜″	50′	72′	overhand
1949	10″	55′	72′	overhand
1950	10″	55′	72′	overhand
1951	10″	55′	72′	overhand
1952	10″	55′	72′	overhand
1953	10″	56′	75′	overhand
1954	9¼″	60′	85′	overhand

Dorothy Kamenshek

THE STREAMLINER WHICH BORE SIX YOUNG BALLPLAYERS
from Cincinnati to Chicago in May 1943 was named the *James
Whitcomb Riley*. En route to Wrigley Field, Dorothy Kamenshek
and her five companions must have talked about many things:
What was this "girls' baseball league"? Who among them would
make the cut? What would it be like playing professional baseball
120 games a year?

Dottie Kamenshek had little way of knowing that she would
become the best player in the history of the All-American Girls
Baseball League. Like most of the young women signed to the
league its first year, she grew up playing softball, not baseball.
Born December 21, 1925, she was seventeen years old, falling
just short of the median age range (18–22) of the first year's players. Standing five feet, six inches tall and weighing 135 pounds,
she was at the upper limit of the average height and weight range.

At Wrigley Field, with the rain pouring down and tryouts taking
place under the stands, Dottie was distraught to discover that
somebody had stolen her only glove, an outfielder's model. Coming from a poor family (her father died when she was nine), she
must have wondered how she could ever afford another. Maybe

she wished she had persuaded her mother into letting her join the army as a way of making money and learning a skill. But Mrs. Kamenshek had firmly refused the army option, and had allowed her daughter to travel to Chicago only because she was convinced Dottie wouldn't be chosen for the new baseball league.

More than 250 women were invited to the Wrigley Field tryouts that first year. And then the cuts began. "They started weeding people out almost the first day. You'd be afraid to answer the phone in your hotel room," recalls Kamenshek. But two Cincinnati women made the final sixty—Betsy Jochum and Dottie Kamenshek. Assigned to the South Bend (Ind.) Blue Sox, Betsy went on a slugging spree that earned her the nickname Sockum Jochum. Dottie went to the Rockford (Ill.) Peaches, where her teammates promptly dubbed her Kammie to distinguish her from two other Dotties on the team.

Manager Eddie Stumpf put Kammie in the outfield because that's where she had played in an industrial softball league, but after a dozen games he told the left-hander to play first base. Although a naturally good fielder and hitter, Kamenshek was the kind of person who wanted to learn more and do better.

The Rockford fans, possibly the most enthusiastic and supportive in the league, didn't recognize the cream of the crop that first year. When two All-Star teams of AAGBLers were chosen to play the first night game ever held in Wrigley Field on July 1, 1943, Rockford fans did not choose Dorothy Kamenshek. No matter: by the time the league got around to choosing an All-Star team in 1945, they chose Kammie for first base—that year and each succeeding year.

Dorothy Kamenshek, Rockford Peaches

"A girl baseball star who has been called
one of the greatest defensive first basemen—man or woman—of all time, who
has been honored by sports writers all
over the nation, and whose diamond services have been sought by professional
baseball, was honored by the folk in her
adopted home town Saturday night.

"More than 3,000 baseball fans
braved the frigid temperatures to pay
tribute to the Rockford Peaches' Dottie
Kamenshek. It was 'Kamenshek Night' in
Beyer Stadium.

"In one of the most successful celebrations ever held in Rockford to honor an
athlete, Miss Kamenshek was presented
with $789.69 in contributions from the
fans. She also received a $50 war bond
from her teammates, another $50 war
bond from her mother, and hundreds of
other gifts, ranging from an electric cook-
er to a corsage, from friends and fans.

"A truck was needed to carry the mass
of gifts away from the stadium."

—*Rockford Star*, August 20, 1950

Singular fielding was what set Kamenshek apart from all other
first sackers. Wally Pipp, former first-baseman for the New York
Yankees, declared she was the "fanciest-fielding first baseman
I've ever seen, man or woman." Because the throws from the second baseman, the shortstop, and the third baseman don't arrive at
first base in the same air lane, a first baseman has to keep her foot
on the bag and stretch in every direction. Peaches teammate Rose
Gacioch believes that "Kammie was ahead of her time. She used
to make the split at first base the way they do in the majors now.
It's like they learned from her."

By nature a fine athlete, Kamenshek made herself even better
through hard work. "I practiced my footwork in winter on a
pillow," she explains. "I threw it on the floor in front of a full-
length mirror and pretended the pillow was first base. You try to
make yourself as long as possible. I practiced shifting my feet. I
stayed flexible year-round." She also studied major league first
basemen, watching their footwork. When spring training rolled
around, Kammie was always ready.

This fancy-fielding player was also an outstanding contact hitter, a Ty Cobb type who could put the wood on the ball and
scratch out a hit when her team needed it the most. In 1945 the
Peaches were engaged in a semifinal playoff series against the
Grand Rapids (Mich.) Chicks to determine who would face the
Fort Wayne (Ind.) Daisies in the Shaughnessy Series (the AAGBL
equivalent of the World Series). As the *Rockford Register Republic*
reported, "Kamenshek, who has batted .571 and played errorless
ball in two playoff games to date, was the sparkplug of the Rockford attack last night. She scored twice, got two singles, a triple

and a walk in four trips to the platter, and dug many a poor throw out of the dirt at first to bottle up the Grand Rapids offensive." Behind the pitching of Carolyn Morris, the bat and glove of Dorothy Kamenshek, and great plays by the entire team, the Rockford Peaches went on to beat Fort Wayne and claim their first Shaughnessy Series title.

The caliber of Rockford ballplaying had improved midway through the 1944 season, when Bill Allington took over as manager. From then on the Peaches couldn't hang around on the tree ripening at leisure: Allington drilled them with baseball history, baseball facts, baseball rules, and baseball plays—in the dugout, after the game, on the team bus. Although Allington worked them to the extreme, he believed that some players might want even more help. If so, he was there to give it.

And Dottie was there to take it. Every day, Allington would position a handkerchief along the third base line where a good bunt would drop. He would position another one along the first base line. Kammie would learn to drop a bunt in exactly that place. She could drive the ball to the outfield, too, pulling it or hitting to the opposite field. Jean Faut, the dominant pitcher of the league's overhand era, says of Kamenshek, "She was a great hitter. The free swingers were not too bad for me to handle, but she was a punch hitter and she gave me a lot of trouble."

Although the baseball world was awed by Kammie's fine fielding, she is proudest of her hitting, and in baseball it was the hitters she admired most. Once she took a bus from Cincinnati to Detroit just to see Ted Williams play. "It was one of my greatest thrills," she remembers. Her favorite player of all time was Stan

Kammie at first base

Musial. Like her hero, she stood deep in the box in order to see the pitch the longest possible time.

In 1946, Dorothy Kamenshek won the All-American Girls Baseball League batting title with a .316 average, and in 1947 she took it again by hitting .306. In those dead-ball days, these were high averages. Of all long-time league players, she had the highest lifetime batting average, .292. In 3,736 at-bats, she struck out only eighty-one times. As the AAGBL ball became smaller and livelier, Kammie's yearly averages went up—.334 in 1950, .345 in 1951. A player who lived to hit, she must have experienced a wonderful thrill when the red-seamed 10⅜-inch ball was introduced in 1948. The first league ball that didn't have a plastic center, it emitted a loud crack as it came off the bat.

So great a player was this Rockford Peach that the minor league Fort Lauderdale club of the Florida International League tried to buy her contract. But not only would the AAGBL not give up Kammie's contract, she herself distrusted the Fort Lauderdale offer, believing it was designed only "to draw in an audience," not to get women into baseball. "I didn't want to be a guinea pig," she says, "so I turned the offer down."

National Baseball Hall of Fame exhibit

Peaches fans admired their first baseman so much that in 1950 they held a "Kamenshek Night" to honor her. Personal friends, family members, teammates, and fans attended, bearing so many gifts that a truck had to haul them away. Asked to comment on the event, Manager Bill Allington told reporters that his first baseman "had a good cry and three hits." Asked if she cried in baseball, Kammie admits it. "I'm sentimental," she confesses.

Kamenshek retired in January 1952 after nine full seasons of play. The game to which Kammie had given so much gave her the courage and confidence to move on to another full-time career. While still playing for the Peaches, she began to attend the University of Cincinnati during the off-season. There she majored in physical education, although she had the feeling that it wasn't quite right for her. When she injured her back in 1949 (and wore a back brace while playing) and encountered physical therapy, she knew she had found her second calling. Switching to Marquette University, she continued her education and graduated in 1958, at the age of thirty-two.

After a few years as a physical therapist in Michigan, Kamenshek moved to California in 1961. There she became chief of the Los Angeles Crippled Children's Services Department. Her conscientiousness and hard work won her honors, as it had in baseball. "I ended up in the *Orange County Who's Who* for work in physical therapy," she says. "I'm just as proud of that as I am of my baseball. One thing about our league: it gave a lot of us the courage to go on to professional careers at a time when women didn't do things like that."

THE TEAMS OF THE AAGBL

Years	Teams	City
1943–54	Peaches	Rockford, Illinois
1943–54	Blue Sox	South Bend, Indiana
1943–50	Belles	Racine, Wisconsin
1951–52		Battle Creek, Michigan
1953		Muskegon, Michigan
1943–51	Comets	Kenosha, Wisconsin
1944	Chicks	Milwaukee, Wisconsin
1945–54		Grand Rapids, Michigan
1944	Millerettes/	Minneapolis, Minnesota
1945-54	Daisies	Fort Wayne, Indiana
1946–50	Lassies	Muskegon, Michigan
1951–54		Kalamazoo, Michigan
1946–51	Redwings	Peoria, Illinois
1948	Colleens	Chicago, Illinois
1948	Sallies	Springfield, Illinois

Winter and Wisniewski

As the AAGBL evolved, the baseball records of
Joanne Winter and Connie Wisniewski skewed in opposite directions. The record lines of these two softball pitchers started at
opposite ends of the won-lost column, coincided at victory's peak
in 1946, and when overhand pitching replaced underhand in the
critical year of 1948, diverged once again. One player adapted to
overhand pitching on the mound, the other at the plate.

Joanne Winter's mother died when she was ten, and Joanne
and her brother, John, were raised by their father, who at one time
had them living above a gym while John trained to be a boxer.
Describing herself as someone who "always liked to run, jump,
and holler," Jo loved living in a gym, and, particularly, learning
how to punch the bag and make it roll. Born November 24, 1924,
she was playing softball for thirty-five cents a game by the time
she was twelve, and when the family moved from Maywood,
Illinois, to Chicago, she pitched warmup games before teams of
the National Girls Baseball League took the field. Despite its
name, the NGBL always played softball, and as a softball league
it would prove to be a thorn in the side of the AAGBL, vying with
the latter for players. Before the demise of the All-American Girls

Baseball League at the end of the 1954 season, both Joanne Winter and Connie Wisniewski would play softball for the National Girls Baseball League.

When Winter's brother enlisted in the service during World War II, she convinced her father to move to Arizona so she could try out for the Phoenix Queens or the Ramblers, two nationally prominent women's softball teams. "I learned how to drive a car on the way out," she says. In Arizona the Ramblers accepted her but confined her to the bench while others pitched.

Around the time that Jo, five feet, seven inches tall and weighing 138 pounds, was fidgeting on the bench, she received a telegram from Johnny Gottselig. A star for the Chicago Blackhawks hockey team, Gottselig was, of all things, manager of the 1943 Racine AAGBL team. The telegram offered Jo a contract of $75 a week if she would come to Racine and pitch.

"The wire came and I took off," she remembers. After two days and two nights on a troop-filled train, she reached Chicago, went to the Wrigley Building to get her orders, and arrived in Racine ready to take the mound. In the past the Belle City had hosted a minor league ball team called the Belles, and now the same name was given its entry in Philip K. Wrigley's new softball league.

Pitching for the Racine Belles that first year, Joanne Winter started twenty-nine games and compiled an 11–11 record. Although she came to bat only eighty-three times, she hit twenty-nine singles and one home run, batting a respectable .253. While her pitching record was only fifty-fifty, Winter's identification with the league and camaraderie with her teammates was total. When the Belles defeated the Kenosha Comets in the first championship

Joanne Winter during AAGBL underhand era

Winter during AAGBL overhand era

series at the end of the season, she was so excited that she wired home to her father, "We won the World Series!"

It was extremely disheartening for Winter when in 1944 she went 15–23 in forty starts, recording the most losses in the league that year. She was hurling the kind of pitches she had thrown in all her softball experience, pitches she describes as "feeble underhand like the figure eight." Nor was she satisfied with the speed of her pitches, and it was obvious that in the unique AAGBL game (called "baseball" by late 1944), the opponents were hitting her all over Horlick Field. The next year Winter started thirty-four games and posted a 7–22 record, once again chalking up the most losses in the league.

Understandably discouraged, Jo returned to Arizona and told her father she was going to quit the game. But her father suggested she get help from Nolly Trujillo, a Phoenix softball pitcher whose specialty was the rise ball delivered in the slingshot manner: underhand with minimal windup. "So I adapted," she says, "and adopted a new delivery, the slingshot." Not that easily, of course. Winter spent hours of every day down at the fire station where Trujillo worked while he taught her his rise ball and his catcher caught her attempts. She'll never forget the elation they all felt when, "One day I got it to really shoot and rise and the catcher said, 'Hey, that's it!'"

With the new delivery, everything changed for "the stately righthander," as the Belles program referred to her. At spring training, without telling catcher Irene Hickson what was coming, Jo threw her new rise ball. Hickson leaped into the air to save the pitch. "Hey, what was that?" she demanded. Replied Winter, "That's my new pitch."

In 1946, armed with a slingshot delivery and rise ball, Winter went 33–10 and struck out 183 batters, more than three times her previous high. The victories set a league record, shared by Connie Wisniewski. But Winter also hurled a phenomenal sixty-three consecutive shutout innings. That shutout record still stands today, and Joanne Winter's picture is posted next to it in the National Baseball Hall of Fame display case. Helping pitch the Racine Belles to the Shaughnessy Series championship that year gave her additional glory.

Unfortunately for the softball pitchers in the AAGBL, sidearm pitching was introduced in 1947, and if a pitcher wanted to stay ahead of the now more-sophisticated batters, she had better learn the new delivery. Many pitchers attempted it, but few succeeded. The delivery was difficult to master, and umpires had a hard time determining if a pitch was legal (that is, if it truly came in sidearm, and not overhand). Winter refused to pitch sidearm. "I'd spent my time cultivating this great underhand pitch," she explains. "I stuck in with the underhand." Posting a 22–13 record, she did very well. But the future was staring the league in the face, and the future was overhand.

The woman who learned to drive on the way to Arizona figured she could learn to pitch overhand during the off-season. With the aid of Belle manager Leo Murphy, who had spent one season in the majors but many seasons as a catcher for the minor league Racine Belles, Jo spent the off-season in a gym, learning how to

Phoenix City Golf Champion Joanne Winter, 1960

throw overhand. Both she and Murphy were well satisfied with her mastery of overhand pitching. But when she got to spring training, she developed intense back pain. Doctors recommended an operation, but Jo refused. Instead, she had her back taped before every game, then went out and pitched. By the eighth or ninth inning, she was always in pain. "It was dramatically tougher on me," she says of overhand pitching.

Yet she persisted, and she closed 1948 with a 25–13 record, tying for the league high for wins that year. (Alice Haylett of the Grand Rapids Chicks also won twenty-five games, losing five.) In that first year of overhand pitching, the pitchers had the advantage: batters weren't used to the angle at which the pitches came in and so couldn't pick up clues as to where the ball would cross the plate. With overhand, the curves broke more sharply, fooling the batters. In every way, 1948 was a pitcher's year.

By the following season, the hitters had had a year to look at the stuff and started catching up to the pitchers. Winter started thirty-two games in 1949, winning eleven and losing thirteen. Her hitting, which had been good for a pitcher, showed the effects of overhand pitching on those who seldom saw it from the plate. In sixty-six at-bats she garnered a meager six hits, all of them singles, for a batting average of .091.

Winter's batting average wasn't the only thing declining that year. All over the league, attendance was falling off dramatically. In Racine, one of the smallest of the league cities to begin with, the fall was especially dramatic. At the end of the 1950 season, the Belles folded. That was when Joanne Winter went back to softball, pitching for the Admiral Music Maids of the National

Girls Baseball League in Chicago. After a few years, she called it quits with softball and spent all her time in Arizona, where she taught tennis at the Arizona Biltmore and took up golf. Within a few years she went professional, winning the Phoenix city golf championship in 1959 and 1960 and the Arizona state golf championship in 1962. A founder of the Arizona Silver Belle Championship Golf Tournament and the Diamonds in the Rough Golf School in Payson and Scottsdale, Winter still lives and works in Arizona.

Rookie Connie Wisniewski, Milwaukee Chicks, 1944

Like Joanne Winter, Connie Wisniewski grew up playing softball. Born in Detroit, she had never heard of the AAGBL when it was first started and didn't learn about it until 1944, when a scout spotted her playing softball and signed her. Even though Connie, born on February 18, 1922, was certainly of legal age, she asked her mother's blessing to join the All-American Girls Baseball League. But her mother believed that "only bad girls leave home," and refused to give it. "Okay," said Connie, "then I'll join the army and be gone for four years." Deciding that baseball was the lesser of these two evils, Mrs. Wisniewski gave her blessing and the five-foot, eight-inch, 147-pound Connie joined the Milwaukee Chicks, one of the two expansion teams formed in the league's second year.

And what a year. The Chicks, managed by the great Max Carey, played in Bouchert Stadium, home of the Milwaukee Brewers, when that minor league team wasn't in town. Brewer owner Bill Veeck was one of only two minor league owners who allowed Wrigley to use their stadiums for women to play "girls' baseball," the other being the owner of the Minneapolis Millers. Playing in

Bouchert thrilled Wisniewski, who had grown up a baseball fan and used to stand outside Briggs Stadium in Detroit, waiting to catch foul balls and get into the game free. Her heroes were Charlie Gehringer and Hank Greenberg, but she was thrilled when Casey Stengel, manager of the Brewers, invited her to sit in the dugout with him and Carey one time.

What got Connie that invitation, aside from the fact that she was affable and a baseball fan, was that her pitching was tearing

JUNIOR BELLES

Under the sponsorship and guidance of the Racine Belles, a Junior Belles program for girls who wanted to play AAGBL-style baseball was started in 1947, with more than 100 girls attending tryouts. Sixty were chosen to play on one of four Junior Belles teams—the Grays, Greens, Reds, and Golds. Each team was managed by a man with previous baseball experience who reported to Belles manager Leo Murphy.

The Junior Belles wore the AAGBL-style uniform—a dress, knee-high stockings, and a baseball cap. Unlike the league caps, which usually bore the first letter of a team's city within a circle (R for Racine, SB for South Bend), the Junior Belles' caps were plain. Coached by their managers,

the girls learned the fundamentals of baseball: batting styles, how to play individual positions, how to throw, and how (and why) to interpret baseball signs.

In 1948, even more girls flocked to tryouts than in 1947. Although the Junior Belles started by playing high-scoring, double-digit games, by the time their short season ended they were staging close contests of 2–1 or 1–0. To the thrill of the juniors and the delight of fans, Junior Belles occasionally played exhibition games in Horlick Field before the Racine Belles began their game. So popular were the Junior Belles that they even traveled within Wisconsin, giving exhibition games.

A few of the other AAGBL teams, in combination with the cities they played

in, sponsored junior teams, among them the Lassies and the Comets. It was the hope of both the AAGBL management and the cities which sponsored teams that the junior program would prove so successful that it would spread across the state, involving thousands of girls in baseball games that might culminate in a state championship. From these junior players, the AAGBL hoped to draw future big leaguers.

That never happened, for with the lessening attendance at AAGBL games, the money available for junior girls baseball was harder to come by. At the end of the 1950 season, the Racine Belles folded, and along with them, the Junior Belles.

up the league. As a rookie she won her first five games, then injured her knee and had to wear a knee brace the rest of the season. When a ball was hit her way, she could field it only by throwing herself on the ground. The rangy right-hander ended every game with the dirtiest uniform imaginable. By season's end she had a 23–10 record and the highest winning percentage in the league.

Throwing right but batting left, Wisniewski wasn't as good a hitter as Winter. In her 111 at-bats, she collected only seventeen hits for an anemic but pitcher-acceptable .153. Pitchers weren't there to hit, anyway, and nobody thought twice about it—especially when Connie's courage and talent won all four playoff games at season's end, giving the Milwaukee Chicks the 1944 championship.

Despite the support of luminaries such as Wrigley, Veeck, and Carey, and despite the great pitching of Wisniewski and the brilliant baseball playing of Chicks such as Dorothy "Mickey" Maguire, Ernestine "Teeny" Petras, Doris Tetzlaff, Betty Whiting, Alma "Ziggy" Ziegler, Thelma "Tiby" Eisen, and Merle Keagle, the Milwaukee fans weren't interested in the idea of women playing baseball of any kind. Attendance was sparse, and at the end of the season the Chicks franchise was moved.

Finding themselves in Grand Rapids, Michigan, the next year, the Chicks were at first afraid the Christian citizens wouldn't like them because they played ball on Sunday. But the citizens gobbled up the season tickets, and those who wouldn't attend Sunday games gave their tickets to those who would. In 1945, Connie, nicknamed Iron Woman because she once pitched and won both ends of a doubleheader, started forty-six games, ending the season with a 32–11 record and a 0.81 earned run average. So overpowering was her performance on the mound that the AAGBL chose her as its first Player of the Year, presenting her with a large trophy.

Connie topped that performance the next year, when she racked up a .786 winning percentage, her 33–9 record edging out Joanne Winter's 33–10. The Chicks ace also batted .250 in 1946, very high for a pitcher during the league's dead-ball days.

Then came sidearm pitching, and while Winter posted a 22–13 record with underhand delivery in 1947, Wisniewski tried sidearm and ended the season with a 16–14 record. Midway through the season, knowing she couldn't adjust to sidearm pitching, she told a reporter she'd be happy if she won ten games. At the plate, though, sidearm didn't baffle her: in her 189 at-bats she hit .291, improving steadily—unlike Winter, who had started out hitting .253 in 1943 and was down to .162 by 1947.

Not only was sidearm pitching beyond Connie's specific abilities, she knew overhand was, too. "When I tried overhand, the ball would shoot up. Then I tried sidearm again, but hurt my elbow. My arm got sore. I would have walked everybody." Resigned to the fact she couldn't adapt to overhand, Wisniewski informed her manager, "I guess this is my last year."

"I sure could use your bat," replied Johnny Rawlings, who had been an infielder for the Boston Braves and Pittsburgh Pirates. "I hate to think of you quitting. Why don't you play the outfield?"

The suggestion was a lifesaver for the popular player. As her at-bats increased, her hitting improved. Wisniewski adapted to overhand pitching not on the mound but at the plate, smashing 127 hits (twenty doubles, two triples, and a year-high seven home runs) in 1948. Batting .289, she was the AAGBL's third best hitter, a valuable asset to her team.

But she had to learn to play the outfield, an unnatural position for her. "The minute it's hit you're supposed to be going. I didn't have the natural instinct for the outfield, to go in or out with the ball," she says. "I couldn't tell." Rawlings put Wisniewski in right field, where center fielder Merle "Pat" Keagle helped her out. "Pat Keagle would come into right field shouting, 'I've got it!' I would say, 'Pat, if you can get it, just come in. I'll move over for you.'" Keagle, at five-foot-two and 144 pounds, was a stalwart player. Connie remembers that, "Once Pat was yelling, 'I've got it! I've got it!' and I said, 'Pat, how the hell can you—it's in my glove?'" The next thing Connie remembered was, "I thought a Mack truck hit me: it was Pat barreling into me, trying to get the ball."

Connie Wisniewski, Grand Rapids Chicks

With Keagle's help, and sometimes despite it, Wisniewski improved in the outfield. At the plate she hit .326 in 1951, again the third highest in the league. She was chosen as an All-Star outfielder in 1948 and 1949 and again in 1951 and 1952.

In 1949 the National Girls Baseball League offered Connie $500 a week if she would quit the AAGBL and finish the season with the NGBL. She said no, but added, "See me next year." Offered $250 a week in 1950, Wisniewski jumped to the NGBL, mainly as a protest against the severe wage cuts AAGBL players were being forced to take. But she disliked the NGBL, particularly for what she considered its lack of professionalism and the gamblers who seemed to hang around the teams. When the Chicks matched her NGBL salary in 1951, she returned to the AAGBL. "In the league it was all nonprofit. There were controls and everything was under one management," she explains. "We played by baseball rules and we had top-notch managers. It was a first-class operation [and] it was expected we would abide by the rules."

The following year Wisniewski turned thirty and decided it was time to retire. She had been working at General Motors during the off-seasons, on aircraft during the war and on Buicks afterward. "I thought maybe some not good years were coming up," she says, referring to her playing skills. "Ziggy [Alma Ziegler] was called 'Grandma' by some players. I wanted to go out on top." So she quit the league and worked full-time at GM. "But I had no idea it wouldn't last. I joined the fan club after I quit."

When the AAGBL folded at the end of the 1954 season, Wisniewski's life, like that of the other players, went on in other directions. After she retired from General Motors she moved to Florida, where she attends minor league games and golfs. She remembers her baseball years with enthusiasm, not just for the ball games but for the camaraderie and the new friends made. "I could crisscross America and Canada and know someone in practically every state and province," she says.

Both Winter and Wisniewski had the ability and willpower to adapt. Because playing the game meant so much to them, they overcame pain, distance, and radical change to survive and excel in AAGBL baseball.

The Minneapolis Millerettes

AFTER 1960, EXPANSION TEAMS BEGAN POPPING UP IN the major leagues like pingos in artificial turf: Kansas City, Houston, Seattle, Anaheim, San Diego, Denver, Miami, and even New York City. The most infamous expansion team of all, the New York Mets, posted a 40–120 record their first year and dwelt in the cellar of the National League for so long that their coming to life in 1969 gave rise to the name "Miracle Mets." The Minneapolis Millerettes were never that bad.

In 1944, only the second year of the All-American Girls Baseball League, Philip K. Wrigley added two new teams to the original four. Although the AAGBL had proved successful in midsized towns such as Racine, Wisconsin, and Rockford, Illinois, Wrigley wanted it to prosper in large cities. Before tackling Chicago itself, the league expanded to Minneapolis and Milwaukee. The Minneapolis Millerettes were managed by Claude "Bubber" Jonnard, who had pitched for the New York Giants. At the helm of the Milwaukee Chicks was Max Carey, who had been a leading base-stealer and hitter with the Pittsburgh Pirates and who would be elected to the Hall of Fame in 1961.

The Minneapolis roster was full of first-year players, four of

"In a setting of continuous soprano and contralto chatter, the Rockford Peaches uncurled the Minneapolis nine in the All American Girls Professional ball opening at Nicollet Park Saturday, 5 to 4.

"But that chatter was the only feminine touch to the proceedings. In a welter of flaring skirts, headlong and feet-first slides into base, bodily contact, good pitching and really brilliant outfielding, [Rockford] won by great defensive work after capturing a mid-game lead when the Millerette defense sprang a temporary weakness."

—Halsey Hall, *The Minneapolis Tribune*, May 28, 1944

them from the sunny climate of Southern California. There Dorothy Wiltse, Lavonne "Pepper" Paire, Faye Dancer, and Annabelle Lee had played professional softball before crowds as large as thirty thousand. The "California girls," as they were called, exuded great confidence and struck some as downright cocky. A few of the rookies were from Canada, notably the Callaghan sisters, Helen and Margaret. Lorraine Borg and Peggy Torrison were local players—Minneapolis softball stars whom the league signed to help draw crowds.

The Millerettes schedule was coordinated with that of the minor league Millers so that both could use Nicollet Park. Scheduled for Saturday, May 27, the women's home opener against the

Minneapolis Millerettes, 1944

Rockford Peaches was covered in the sports pages, which reported on pregame ceremonies (music, a parade, and a flag raising) and on local heroes Borg and Torrison, scheduled to catch and play third, respectively.

Although the Millerettes lost the first game, 5–4, the caliber of play was so much better than expected that sportswriter Halsey Hall gave praise where it was due. Sunday's doubleheader was split with the Peaches, the Millerettes winning the first, 7–6, and losing the second, 2–0. A sign of coming trouble was the fact that five of the Peaches' six runs in the first game were the result of Millerette errors.

Several games later, the expansion team hit the road. Two weeks into the season, the South Bend Blue Sox were in first place with a 10–5 record; Minneapolis occupied second at 9–6. Back in the Twin Cities, the press reported briefly on the road games, tagging the team the "challenging Minneapolis Millerettes."

Not for long. Just six days later, the northernmost team sank to fourth place in a six-team league.

On June 17 the Millerettes started another home stand. Led by the sterling pitching of Dottie Wiltse, they held the Racine Belles hitless for the first 10⅔ innings but lost the fifteen-inning thriller, 3–2. Knocking out fourteen hits, Minneapolis left twenty-two runners stranded. So many of the team's games were going into extra innings that the press hung a new label on the club: the "Marathon Millerettes." In addition to committing abundant errors, the Millerettes were unable to bring runners home. Still the young players fought on. With great hitting from Helen

Callaghan and Faye Dancer, and valiant pitching from Dottie Wiltse, the expansion team compiled a 14–14 record by the end of the third week.

Equilibrium seldom lasts long. On June 21, the Blue Sox pounded the Millerettes, 7–1. Blowing an early lead the following day, Minneapolis again lost to the Sox. Facing the Kenosha Comets next, the team suffered its fifth and sixth consecutive losses and on June 26 dropped a doubleheader. The next day Peggy Torrison and Lorraine Borg quit the league to rejoin their amateur softball team, which was vying for first place in the city league.

Unimpeded by the loss of the softball players, the Millerettes won two games in a row, then began a protracted losing streak. When Wiltse walked eight batters in one game, the press began to complain that opponents were winning on fewer hits than the Millerettes. As a team, the Millerettes just couldn't jell.

The Fourth of July holiday resulted in more duds: two to the Milwaukee Chicks on July 2, one to the Chicks the next day, and two more to the Chicks on July 4. On July 5 the Millerettes dropped to the cellar in league standings.

Heavy rain in the Twin Cities caused postponement of the July 6 game, requiring the marathoners to play two games on Friday night, two on Saturday, and two more on Sunday. In the first doubleheader, "The Racine Belles jumped all over Dottie Wiltse, Millerettes' ace hurler . . . to win 4–2, and came back in the nightcap to belt Annabelle Lee for 12 hits and a 6–3 victory. . . ."

Pounded to pieces at home, the Millerettes left town on July 17 for a four-week trip. In Milwaukee the Chicks eked out a 2–1 victory over their sister expansion team on a squeeze bunt with two out in the bottom of the ninth. But on July 21 the Millerettes clobbered the Chicks, 9–1, with Annabelle Lee hurling an excellent game and Helen Callaghan going 3-for-3, including a long home run.

The victory was insufficient to forestall the future. On July 23 the *Minneapolis Tribune* carried the news: "Millerettes Lost to City Rest of Year." According to the story, "Ken Sells, president of the circuit, announced shortly after a conference in the city Saturday that Minneapolis' representative will retain that name for the balance of the season, but will play as a road team exclusively.

"This action was taken after four independent clubs in the league—Racine, Kenosha, Rockford and South Bend—objected to making the trip to Minneapolis because of the heavy traveling expenses with such small crowds attending the games." After this account, the Minneapolis papers carried no further news of the team that bore the city name.

Outcasts, doomed to wander like Ishmael, the Millerettes were now tagged the "Orphans." The players remember that the clothes they left behind in Minneapolis had to be replaced on the never-ending road trip. As orphans, the team played no worse than it had before: possibly a bit better. On July 29, Annabelle Lee hurled the AAGBL's first perfect game, an 18–0 gem against the Kenosha Comets.

When the long season ended in September, the Millerettes sat in the cellar with a 45-72 record. But their potential showed. Dottie Wiltse, who hit forty-four batters (thus setting a league record), at least emerged with twenty wins and sixteen losses.

Pitcher Dorothy Wiltse Collins of Fort Wayne Daisies

1944 AAGBL Standings

Team	W	L	Pct.
Milwaukee Chicks	70	45	.609
South Bend Blue Sox	64	52	.552
Kenosha Comets	62	54	.534
Rockford Peaches	53	60	.469
Racine Belles	53	64	.453
Minneapolis Millerettes	45	72	.385

Helen Callaghan, who stood five-foot-one and weighed 105 pounds, batted .287 (second highest in the league), stole 112 bases, and scored eighty-one runs.

That winter, the Orphans learned that Fort Wayne, Indiana, would be their new home. There they became the Fort Wayne Daisies, and there they stayed—a much-loved and greatly appreciated team. As the Daisies, they became challengers, more often in seasonal playoffs than not.

Ironically, the Milwaukee Chicks, the other expansion team of 1944, went all the way to the top under Max Carey's management, winning the championship series, four games to three. The city of Milwaukee was not impressed. The Chicks, too, were told to leave town, and Grand Rapids, Michigan, became their new home. Wrigley's attempt to bring women's baseball to large cities was laid to rest until 1948, when the league tried to expand into Chicago and Springfield, Illinois.

Pitcher Dorothy Wiltse moved to Fort Wayne with the Daisies and there met Harvey Collins, who asked her out after he saw her pitch a doubleheader. Wiltse's 1945 record on the Fort Wayne Daisies was 29–10, with a 0.83 ERA and a record seventeen shutouts. In 1946 she struck out 294 batters, setting another record. She married Collins, and as Dorothy Wiltse Collins continued to pitch impressively, even when six months pregnant. Daisy fans would ask for autographs; florists delivered roses when she pitched a shutout. She played a key role in helping to form the AAGBL Players Association and today functions as its newsletter editor and spokesperson.

Outfielder Helen Callaghan also moved to Fort Wayne with the team and in 1945 led the league in batting with a .299 average. After the 1948 season, she quit to raise a family. One of her five sons, Kelly Candaele, wrote *A League of Their Own,* the documentary that inspired the Penny Marshall film of the same title. Youngest son Casey Candaele is a major-leaguer. Helen Callaghan St. Aubin died in 1992.

Catcher Ruth Lessing went to the Daisies, then was traded to the Chicks in 1946. She played out the rest of her career in Grand Rapids, retiring in 1949. Elected to the All-Star teams in 1946–48, she holds several league records for catchers: most games played in a season (125 in 1948), most assists (141), and most put-outs (634).

Annabelle Lee also went to Fort Wayne, then to the Peoria Redwings and then the Grand Rapids Chicks. She continued to play in the league until 1950. Her nephew, Bill "Spaceman" Lee, pitched for the Montreal Expos and the Boston Red Sox in the 1970s and '80s and credits his aunt with teaching him how to pitch. Spaceman accompanied Annabelle to Cooperstown when the AAGBL was given a display in the Baseball Hall of Fame in 1988.

Ruth "Tex" Lessing

Rose Gacioch

WHEN ROSE GACIOCH JOINED THE ALL-AMERICAN GIRLS Baseball League in 1944, she was twenty-eight years old. For the next eleven years she would play side-by-side with women 10–20 years her junior. As the game's softball layers were peeled away and only hardball remained, "Rockford Rosie" would prove steady and reliable—a worthy link between the great tradition of bloomer girl baseball and the well-paid and well-played AAGBL.

Born August 31, 1915, in Wheeling, West Virginia, Rose was the youngest of four children. Her father died before she was born and her mother remarried when Rose was two or three. She grew up poor but happy, enjoying swimming in the Ohio River and playing baseball. Engrossed with the game, Rose once skipped school to see Babe Ruth and Lou Gehrig, knowing she would be whipped when she got home. She was, but she never regretted it. In a dispute over batting order with an older sister she adored, she gave her sister a black eye.

Like many a kid taken with the national pastime, Rose practiced on her own. She explains how she learned to pitch: "I lived on a hillside and there were two trees in a row. I threw the ball at them and tried to make it curve between the two trees."

With the help of a friend named Jane and an old mattress, she continued to experiment. Jane would stand behind the mattress to hold it up and Rose would fire baseballs at it. Then they cut a hole in the mattress and Rose practiced throwing the ball through the hole. After she mastered that, she drew arrows to the left and right of the hole and practiced inside and outside pitches.

When Gacioch was fifteen years old, her mother died. Living with an aunt and uncle, Rose got a job in a corrugating plant whose president, Jack Felton, happened to watch her play baseball and happened to know Maud Nelson. Felton wrote to Nelson, who gave Rose a tryout and added her to the All Star Ranger Girls as pitcher and outfielder.

Unfortunately for Rose Gacioch and other young players, 1934 was the last year of bloomer girl baseball, and after it was gone women who wanted to play the diamond game had to play softball. Gacioch learned how to play that game when "Sad Sam" Jones, former major-leaguer, introduced her to barnstorming softball. Soon she was playing weekend games in Ohio and Pennsylvania, earning as much as $50 for two days' play. She played softball in Duquesne Gardens in Pittsburgh, and later the team traveled to Madison Square Garden, where after a game Cookie Lavagetto of the Brooklyn Dodgers took the players to the World's Fair.

When World War II came, Gacioch was working in a Wheeling factory. She remembers that one day during her lunch break she saw a picture of an AAGBL player in a New York newspaper. "You know," she announced to her lunch companions excitedly, "I'm going to be on that team." Her factorymates pointed out that she was too old to play baseball, but a machinist overheard her and

Rose Gacioch, Rockford Peaches

informed them that his daughter was a chaperone for the South Bend Blue Sox. "I'll have her look you up," he told Rose. A month or so later, the daughter came to Wheeling, gave five-foot-six, 134-pound Rose a tryout, and arranged for her to attend the league's 1944 spring training session in Peru, Illinois. Gacioch made the cut and was assigned to the South Bend Blue Sox.

Bert Niehoff—the man who had sent Jackie Mitchell to the mound to face Ruth and Gehrig in 1931—was managing the Blue Sox that year. "He taught me a lot," recalls Rose. "He knew baseball, just like Bill Allington did. Bert would explain everything to you. He would say to you, 'You used to play shortstop, and this is what you did,' and he'd describe how you played. Then he'd tell you what to change to play the outfield." In South Bend, Niehoff put her in right field. "After Bert taught me how to play the outfield better, I made the second baseman get closer to the infield. I could throw players out from the outfield." Playing right field

Rockford Peaches, Gacioch center

for the Rockford Peaches in 1945, Gacioch set an all-time AAGBL record of thirty-one assists from the outfield.

The story of how Gacioch got from South Bend to Rockford reveals much about league strength and individual prejudices. During the 1943–50 period of management under Philip K. Wrigley and then Arthur Meyerhoff, the AAGBL board of directors sought to build teams of equal strength, so that fans would be treated to close games and last-day pennant races. Theoretical equality was achieved by the reallocation of certain players.

By early 1945 each of the six teams was permitted to retain ten players not subject to trade. The president of the South Bend Blue Sox, a man named Livengood, was sent to Chicago in April 1945 with instructions to retain, among others, Betsy Jochum, Lois Florreich, Dottie Schroeder, Rose Gacioch, Bonnie Baker, and Marge Stefani. Livengood returned from the meeting having traded Gacioch. In writing the history of the Blue Sox years later, Dr. Harold Dailey, a dentist who served on the board and was at one time president of the club, started the section on the 1945 season in this way: "This was by far the most unpleasant season of the history of the club. Many good ballplayers were gotten rid of, the first was that Rose Gacioch was given away in the allocation meeting in Chicago."

When Dailey later learned that "Livengood had given away Gacioch because she used poor English," he helped pass a motion that the team manager, and not the club president, be given full charge of running the team. "The loss of Gacioch was felt for years to come," mourned Dailey. Had Livengood been president of the St. Louis Cardinals, one wonders if he would have traded Dizzy Dean because he "used poor English."

Managed by Bill Allington, the 1945 Rockford Peaches had on their roster such quality players as Olive Little, Jo Lenard, Dottie Kamenshek, Dorothy "Snookie" Harrell, Dottie Ferguson, Carolyn Morris, Millie Deegan, and rookie Jean Cione. Recognizing the strengths of the twenty-nine-year-old Gacioch, Allington put her in right field. In addition to racking up thirty-one assists that year, she belted nine triples and batted in forty-four runs: the triples and RBIs were 1945 league records. In 1946, Gacioch had thirty assists, and in 1947 she tied her own record of thirty-one (a total also achieved by Doris Sams that year). Of her many contributions to the Peaches, Rose is proudest of the assists record, "because that's most important to the team."

During the 1948 season, Allington looked at his thirty-three-

Gacioch at bat, Allington coaching at third

year-old right fielder and commented, "Rose, you used to be a pitcher, didn't you?" Confirming it, Rose waited. "Why don't you go back to pitching?" he suggested, perhaps staring out at the playing field. "Why?" she asked. "I need a pitcher," he replied, "and there's a lot of ground to cover in the outfield, and you're slowing down. There's not so much ground to cover when you pitch."

So Gacioch returned to pitching, posting a 14–5 record and a 2.21 earned run average. She started only fourteen games the next season, winning nine and losing two. Her best year was 1951—with a 20–7 record and a 1.68 ERA, she was the league's only twenty-game winner that season. Gacioch continued to pitch until the league folded, sometimes surprising even herself, as when on August 26, 1953, she hurled a seven-inning no-hitter against South Bend. (In the AAGBL, the first—and sometimes second—game of a doubleheader went only seven innings.)

During the last years of league play, Allington found himself needing a utility infielder, and he naturally turned to Rockford Rosie. When she wasn't pitching, she played third base or first base. In 1952 she was voted to the All-Star team as a pitcher, in 1953 as a utility infielder, and in 1954 again as a pitcher.

When Rose Gacioch had first moved to Rockford, she worked in Detroit during the off-season, running a milling machine for Chrysler Corporation. Soon she became one of the seven or eight Peaches who lived in Rockford year-round. She took up bowling and in 1954, just before the beginning of the league's last season, Gacioch won the national doubles bowling championship with partner Fran Stennett.

Rose retired to Michigan to live near her nieces and nephews and their children. Today she spends a lot of time fishing and continues to bowl in senior tournaments. Her niece took her to the Baseball Hall of Fame for the opening of the Women in Baseball display in 1988, and her grandnephew from Connecticut came down to share the historic moment with her.

The living link between bloomer girl baseball and the women who played in stadiums of their own was strong, vital, and totally reliable. Rose Gacioch, like Maud Nelson, was in it for the long haul.

CANADIAN PEACH

Dorothy Ferguson, champion speed skater and hockey player from Winnipeg, Canada, was recruited by the AAGBL in 1945 and assigned to the Rockford Peaches. Except for one month with the Peoria (Ill.) Redwings in 1946, she was a Peach until the league folded in 1954.

Playing second base for the Peaches, "Fergie" became very popular for her specialty: crowding the plate in such a way that the opposing pitcher had to throw outside pitches and walk her, or throw down the middle and hit her. One way or another, Fergie regularly reached first base. There, she would bend forward so that her pigtails hung loose. "If it was going to be a run-and-hit," she explains, "I'd flip my right pigtail over my shoulder with my right hand. If a hit-and-run was on, then Kammie [Dorothy Kamenshek] would touch the end of her bat while taking practice swings." The other teams never managed to steal the signal. "I was not a great hitter," Fergie says, "but I made it, I guess, because I could run fast and throw hard. And, I liked to win."

The town, the people, and the Peaches appealed to her so much that she stayed in Rockford year-round. So did Don Key, who had followed her down from Winnipeg. After four baseball seasons, they were married early in 1949. The couple settled in Rockford for good, with Fergie playing ball another six years.

In 1946, manager Bill Allington asked Fergie to play center field. She was stunned. "I cried when they asked me if I'd move to the outfield," she recalls. "I thought it was a demotion." A good team player, she took the "demotion" and learned how to patrol the territory. Her speed enabled her to cover a lot of ground, and soon she liked the job so much she couldn't imagine not having responsibility for center field.

"I'd rather play baseball than anything," she says, echoing the words of so many league players. In 1954, when times were so bad that the Peaches couldn't even afford a bus, the players drove their own cars to the games and played without pay at the end of the season. "You loved the game, and it became a way of life."

After the league folded, the Keys had two children, a son and daughter, and raised them in Rockford. The only member of the Peaches who still lives in town, Dottie Ferguson Key attends all the AAGBL reunions and keeps in touch with her former teammates. "My years with the Peaches," she says, "were the best years of my life."

Sophie Kurys

WHEN SHE WAS FOURTEEN YEARS OLD, SOPHIE MARY KURYS of Flint, Michigan, won the Mott Pentathlon for girls with a score of 4,693 out of a possible 5,000—a record that would stand for decades. If an athlete with the speed, aggressiveness, and savvy of Kurys were playing major league baseball today, the manager would have her bat leadoff and steal after she reached base. Johnny Gottselig, hockey-star manager of the Racine Belles, didn't comprehend how exceptional his five-foot-five, 120-pound player was. In 1943 he gave her the sign to steal just often enough to allow her to swipe forty-four bases. The next year Gottselig either got smarter or just looser with the signs. Sophie, playing in 116 games, racked up ninety-six hits, earned sixty-nine walks and was hit by a pitch seven times. Reaching first base 172 times, she stole a phenomenal 166 bases in 1944, seven of them in one game. And that was just the beginning.

Sophie Kurys, Racine Belles second baseman

Along with Joanne Winter, Margaret "Marnie" Danhauser, Edythe Perlick, Irene Hickson, Madeline English, and Eleanor Dapkus, Sophie Kurys was one of the original Racine Belles who stayed with the team throughout its eight-year existence. As rookies the group played so well together that Racine won the AAGBL's first championship series. Although Sophie had played third and shortstop in Flint softball, Gottselig put her in the outfield. When the second baseman was injured after a few games, Kurys took over second and stayed there for the rest of her career.

In 1945 the Belles had a new manager. Although he had spent only part of one year in the majors with Pittsburgh, Leo Murphy had a twenty-five-year career in baseball. It was Murphy who understood that Kurys should be batting leadoff, where more at-bats would increase her chance of getting on base and (inevitably) stealing one or more bags, moving from first to scoring position. Says Kurys, "Johnny Gottselig had me all over the place. Leo Murphy got me to be the leadoff hitter."

In 1945 the "Flint Flash" played in 105 games and reached first base 157 times. Purloining 115 bases, she led the league in steals for the second consecutive year (and every subsequent year she played). "You pretend that you're not taking a big lead," she says of her technique. "I never took a big lead right away. Of course, they knew I was going."

Born May 14, 1925, Sophie turned twenty-one as the 1946 season began. If baseball time can be named by players, then 1946 was the year of Kurys. She played in 113 games, rapped out 112 hits, drew ninety-three walks, and was hit by ten pitches. Reaching base 215 times, she attempted 203 steals, succeeding a monumental 201 times. The Flint Flash was a steady flame, scoring a league-high 117 runs and batting .286, second only to Dottie Kamenshek's .316. Her ninety-three walks also set a league record. That same year she set a .973 fielding record for second base. The 201 stolen bases were not only a record for the year—

Above: Teammates Edie Perlick, Sophie Kurys, Maddy English

Below: Racine Belles, 1947: Kurys, center row, third from left; Leo Murphy, manager

they would remain a league record forever. The second-highest number of steals that year (Tiby Eisen's 128) was less than two-thirds of Sophie's total.

Because Kurys' base-stealing record is unequaled in baseball history (the closest is Rickey Henderson's 130 steals in 1982), the question arises whether her steals were equivalent to major league ones. Did the larger ball and shorter basepaths of the All-American Girls Baseball League give the runner an advantage that major-leaguers don't have? Dr. Robert K. Adair, Sterling Professor of Physics at Yale University, believes it's possible that a runner such as Henderson is at a 0.15-second disadvantage to the pitcher-catcher combination, whereas an AAGBL runner such as Kurys had a 0.04-second advantage over the battery. But Dr. Adair stresses that the microseconds involved are under perfect-play conditions: any variation in running, throwing, and sliding would change the numbers.

As one intimate with the ground, Sophie Kurys judged ballparks from an unusual angle: she was less concerned with the depth of the outfield or smoothness of the infield than with the nature of the dirt. The playing field at Fort Wayne she remembers as the worst in the league, because whenever it rained, the grounds crew burned the field. "To get it playable they put oil and gasoline on it and burned it," she explains. "It was like a brick."

But even on a field merely ground-hard instead of brick-hard, hitting the dirt in a skirt was torture. "They thought that having skirts would show that we were extremely feminine," she says, "but I think all of us would have rather played in standard uniforms." Sliding across the ground in bare skin gave players abrasion upon abrasion: broken skin bled into their clothing and large bruises showed on their legs. "That one year I set the record, my chaperone made this donut affair so the wound wouldn't leak onto my clothes,

because if it did, it would be torture to try and get the clothes off."

As a form of protection, the AAGBL provided players with sliding pads. The women were expected to tape the bulky pads to their thighs, but after trying them, the ballplayers unanimously rejected them. Aside from the fact that the pads looked awful hanging down from a short skirt, "they were too cumbersome," Kurys explains. "So I took them off and took my chances with strawberries. I had strawberries on strawberries. Sometimes now, when I first get up in the morning, I have problems with my thighs."

Kurys is amazed that today some promoters want to start a women's league, "just like ours, skirts and all." She doesn't understand the thinking behind asking anybody to slide in a skirt. If such a league ever does get started, she predicts that "You aren't going to get [today's athletes] to do the things we did. You've got to protect them."

The theoretical 0.04-second advantage wasn't something every league player gained. Only one who could run at the speed of an Olympic athlete and possessed the baseball instincts of a Ty Cobb had this four-hundredths of a second "edge." Maybe it was Sophie Kurys' speed, her uncanny ability to judge the right moment to steal, her admirable aggressiveness in doing so time after time after time, that made her such a great base-stealer. Maybe it was the crowd at the ivy-covered, limestone-walled Horlick Field, cheering her on. Maybe it was the supply of Horlick's malted milk balls in the Belles' dugout. Whatever it was, nobody else in the All-American Girls Baseball League even came close to Kurys' base-stealing achievements: her 201 steals of 1946 and lifetime 1,114 steals in eight years were unrivaled.

The year of Kurys didn't end with Sophie breaking five AAGBL records (walks, steals, runs, fielding, and scoring five runs in one game), for the league-leading Racine Belles faced a best-of-five playoff series against the South Bend Blue Sox and, if they made that, a best-of-seven Shaughnessy Series. Though the Belles didn't know it at the time, their postseason play would start and end in extra-inning symmetry. In their first game against the Blue Sox, the Belles won, 3–2, when Maddy English socked a game-winning double in the bottom of the seventeenth. Racine went on to take the series against South Bend, three games to one.

In the Shaughnessy Series, Racine faced the Rockford Peaches. The Belles won two games at home, then dropped two of the three in Rockford. With the series 3–2 in their favor, the Belles headed home to Horlick Field and the sixth game. Until the seventh game of the 1991 World Series, perhaps no baseball final contest came close to matching the sixth game of the 1946 Shaughnessy Series for sheer drama.

First, there was the pitchers' duel, Rockford's Carolyn Morris against Racine's Joanne Winter. Having her best year ever, Winter had compiled a 33–10 record for the season and pitched a consecutive sixty-three scoreless innings. But as reported by *Major League Baseball Facts and Figures*, the sixth game was a different story: "Winter was in hot water continually and the base paths were constantly clogged with Peaches as the Rockford team garnered 13 hits with never a runner denting the platter and left 19 base runners stranded. Meanwhile, Morris was pitching the masterpiece of them all and at the conclusion of nine innings, there had not been a safe blow by Racine."

In the tenth inning the Belles got to Morris and Bill Allington brought in Millie Deegan to relieve her. Deegan put out the fire in the tenth and the contest continued.

On and on it went, fourteen innings in all. (Although the players all remember it as a fourteen-inning game, *Major League Baseball Facts and Figures* reports it in words as a fourteen-inning game and in line score as a sixteen-inning one.) In the bottom of the fourteenth, Kurys, who had already stolen four bases that night, led off with a single and once again stood on first. "I have a passion for baseball," she says, perhaps explaining what happened. "I like the team concept. You're in there helping each other." So Kurys stole her fifth base. As she watched teammate Betty Trezza at the plate, Sophie found the favorable moment that only she could always find and lit out from second to steal third. At that instant Trezza slapped a short single through the infield.

"A constant, never suspended, physical attitude of alertness was required of every fielder and was supported by continual player 'chatter,' by conference 'huddles,' by signaling and other conventional devices. The girls secured a far superior psychological effect from these devices than is obtained by the average minor league organization. 'Stalling' was minimized; umpire baiting was limited; games (9 innings) seldom consumed more than one hour and 20 minutes. Most important of all was a fast moving procession of what one might call spotlighted episodes subordinate to the game contest. These challenged the attention of the spectator throughout the game. For example if a runner was on a base the spectator was kept on edge by the runner's constant threat to steal. At the same time you were keyed up by the uncertainty of whether the batter would swing, hit-and-run or sacrifice. If two were on bases there was constant maneuvering for a double steal. When long hits inside the park were accomplished most of them involved close plays at second, third or the plate. These plays which gave spectators time to build up suspense-interest through periods ranging from seven to fifteen seconds punctuated every game and held the crowd in breathless suspense as contrasted with synthetic home runs over the fence and their frequent destruction of the suspense period."

—E. W. Moss, *Blue Book Supplement,*
November 1945

Kurys stealing against South Bend Blue Sox, 1947

Glancing at the ball, Kurys touched the bag at third and headed home full speed, knowing her chances of scoring before the ball reached the catcher were questionable.

Throwing herself against the ungiving ground one last time, Kurys caught the plate with a hook slide a fraction of a second before the catcher tagged her, scoring the single run of the game and bringing the victory home to the Belles with her strength and spirit. Swarming across the field, the fans lifted the second baseman and carried her off on their shoulders. "It was such an exciting thing to see Sophie cross that plate," says her best friend and teammate Joanne Winter. "I'll never forget it." Hall-of-Famer Max Carey, president of the All-American Girls Baseball League, was equally excited. "Barring none," he said, "even in the majors, [it's] the best game I've ever seen!"

For her incredible baseball accomplishments, Sophie Kurys was elected the Player of the Year. Not only was she the leading scorer for the season, she was the leading hitter and scorer for the entire postseason series. *Major League Baseball Facts and Figures* assessed her contribution in this way: "She turned more opportunities into runs than any other player in the history of the league."

Kurys went on to play AAGBL baseball for another four years and was elected to the All-Star team four straight seasons, 1946–49. In 1950 she stole 120 bases and hit a year-high seven home runs (tied by Eleanor Callow). When the Racine franchise folded, she went to Chicago to play professional softball for three years. After an additional year of softball in Arizona, she retired from the diamond at the age of thirty-three.

During the off-season, Kurys worked for a Racine manufacturer of electrical automotive and airplane parts. The owner eventually offered her a partnership and she accepted, contributing to the business in a team way by learning all parts and doing all jobs: she worked in manufacturing, quality control, as bookkeeper, a payroll clerk, and in the shipping department. In 1972 she left the business and moved to Arizona.

One thing about Kurys that made her a ballplayer's ballplayer and sets her apart from other masters of the steal such as Rickey Henderson: she never sought to call attention to herself. Even today, if she's being praised, she points out what others have done. Her attitude and personality are best summed up when she talks about her baseball heroes, Charlie Gehringer and, most of all, Hank Greenberg: "They didn't mouth off. They just did the job day in and day out without mouthing off." Sophie Kurys went out and did her job in the same spirit.

The Rockford Peaches

IN STRUCTURING THE ALL-AMERICAN GIRLS BASEBALL
League, Philip K. Wrigley implemented a few concepts that other
baseball barons rejected, one being that ballplayers should be
owned not by individual clubs but by the league as a whole, and
that they should be reallocated as necessary at least once a
season—to ensure close pennant races involving all teams. At the
end of the 1943 season, the Racine Belles finished only one game
ahead of the South Bend Blue Sox and only three games ahead of
the Kenosha Comets. But then came the Rockford Peaches,
throwing Wrigley's theory askew by sitting at the bottom of the
short stack, a full sixteen games out of first and miles out of the
running.

The Rockford Peaches would spend their entire twelve years
of existence throwing league statistics askew, winning four of the
AAGBL's twelve pennants and participating in most of its playoffs. Three factors accounted for the Peaches' success: manager
Bill Allington; fan support; and very good ballplayers who, skilled
in the basics, were able to come through in the clutch.

Bill Allington took over managing the Rockford Peaches
midway through the 1944 season, and although the team ended

AAGBL SERIES CHAMPIONS	
Year	Champions
1943	Racine Belles
1944	Milwaukee Chicks
1945	Rockford Peaches
1946	Racine Belles
1947	Grand Rapids Chicks
1948	Rockford Peaches
1949	Rockford Peaches
1950	Rockford Peaches
1951	South Bend Blue Sox
1952	South Bend Blue Sox
1953	Grand Rapids Chicks
1954	Kalamazoo Lassies

up fourth in a six-team league, its play was so improved and its hopes so high that 3,133 fans braved unseasonably cold weather to attend the Peaches' last home game, on September 5, 1944. There the fans, Allington, and the team all came together at Beyer Stadium (the Peach Orchard, as sportswriters called it) to show the South Bend Blue Sox what the future looked like.

Ever since he had left California for the town on the Rock River, Bill Allington had been grooming his players in the basics of baseball. They responded by playing better and better. That cold September night, ace hurler Carolyn Morris pitched a 9–0 no-hitter against the visiting Blue Sox. Absolutely delighted with one another, fans and Peaches interacted, fans thrusting $1, $5, and $10 bills at players for hits and fielding gems, the Peaches handing out autographed baseballs to fans.

Rockford Peaches, 1945 Shaughnessy Series champions

Fully in charge from the first day of the 1945 season, Allington drilled the women relentlessly in the basics of baseball. A tough manager, he required practice, knowledge, and dedication from his players. Many, such as Dottie Kamenshek and Rose Gacioch, thrived in this atmosphere. A few, such as shortstop Snookie Harrell, resented it. The fact that they all played as a team was a tribute both to their professionalism and his ability to forge a unit out of contrasting parts.

Allington had spent more than twenty years playing in the minors. In 1939 he began coaching women's softball, and in 1944 five of his players tried out for and made the AAGBL. "Bill had a very sarcastic sense of humor," recalls Dottie Wiltse Collins. When she and the four others were leaving California for their Wrigley Field tryouts, they stood at the train station with luggage that held four months of clothing. "My, that's a lot of luggage you're taking for one week," he commented.

Though his humor was sarcastic, Allington always looked out for the welfare of his players. Collins recalls that when she was playing for the Minneapolis Millerettes and Allington was managing the Peaches, she fell in the dugout and broke her tailbone, though she didn't know it at the time. When she took the mound to pitch, it was Allington who stopped the game and asked her what was wrong, and it was he who saw to it that she was taken to the hospital and treated. Rose Gacioch remembers how helpful he was to her, turning her into a pitcher in order to help the Peaches and prolong her career. Allington often did for his players what other managers could have done, but didn't. Wilma Briggs, who played for him when he managed the Fort Wayne Daisies, remembers that on cold days when the players had nothing but cotton jerseys to wear under their ill-suited uniforms, Allington immediately procured wool jerseys for them. In the large concepts and the little details, he went the extra mile.

With the thin, white-haired manager at their helm, the 1945 Peaches—Jo Lenard, Kay Rohrer, Dottie Green, Betty Carveth, Helen Filarski, Dottie Kamenshek, Irene Kotowicz, Alva Jo Fisher, Millie Deegan, Olive Little, Dottie Ferguson, Jean Cione, Carolyn Morris, Rose Gacioch, and Snookie Harrell—blazed through the season with utterly reliable and often spectacular play. Though the lead swung back and forth between Rockford, Fort Wayne, and the Grand Rapids Chicks, the Peaches regained it on August 4 by defeating the Chicks, 1–0, behind the pitching of Olive Little and a booming triple by Deegan that scored Rohrer.

Several days later, Rockford swept the Daisies in Fort Wayne, becoming the only team that year to sweep each opponent in the opponent's home park. On September 1, with four games left to play, the team clinched first place. Throughout the spring and summer, the Rockford newspapers had reported all Peaches games on the front page of the sports section, side-by-side with articles on major league games. Now fans and players were rewarded as the Peaches made their first playoffs.

The first series of games, a best-of-five arrangement, saw first-place Rockford face third-place Grand Rapids and second-place Fort Wayne go against fourth-place Racine. Thanks to the stellar pitching of Carolyn Morris, the hitting of Kamenshek (who at one point was batting 1.000), Gacioch, and Deegan, the Peaches cooped the Chicks. Meanwhile, the Daisies tolled the Belles, making the Shaughnessy Series a Peaches versus Daisies affair.

With the home-field advantage, Rockford took the first two games from the Daisies, 2–1 and 3–2. Play then moved to Fort Wayne, but unstoppable Rockford took the third game, 3–1. Dottie Wiltse, loser of the first game, pitched Fort Wayne to a 2–0 victory in the fourth. But on September 16, 1945, the Peaches won the fifth game 3–2 on a two-run homer by Millie Deegan, winning their first Shaughnessy Series. They repeated in 1948, and in 1949 won an unprecedented third championship (later the Chicks would also win a third).

In 1950 Bill Allington and the Rockford Peaches went after their fourth championship. A few of the 1945 players were still there (Kamenshek, Harrell, Gacioch, and Dottie Ferguson Key), but many had left: Rohrer returned to softball, Little retired to raise a family, and Deegan, Lenard, and Cione had been traded.

The first round of playoffs saw Rockford face Kenosha in Beyer Stadium, where Rockford-born Jean Cione took the mound for the Comets against Rose Gacioch. Around the AAGBL cities, fan

Rose Gacioch, Margaret Wigiser, Bill Allington, Mildred Deegan, Jean Cione

More than thirty-five managers worked for the ten franchises of the All-American Girls Baseball League during its twelve-year existence. Some, such as Eddie Ainsmith, lasted only a month. Others, such as Bill Allington, managed for ten years. At right is a list of the eighteen men who managed league teams for two or more years, along with the teams they managed listed in chronological order. Managers who played in the major leagues are marked with an *, those who played only in the minors with an °.**

attendance had started to decline dramatically in 1949. Rockford, too, felt the decline, though not as severely as Racine, Kenosha, and Peoria. The Peaches were still the pride of the city, the Rockford city vehicle sticker featuring a Peach at bat. The press still gave the Peaches headlines and day-by-day coverage, and reporters at Beyer Stadium described that night's game as a pitchers' duel, with the Peaches jumping off to a 1–0 lead. But in the top of the sixth, Comets Jo Lenard, Fern Shollenberger and Marge Villa loaded the bases. Cione drove them in with a triple, winning her own game.

Rallying, the Peaches won the second game and evened the series. The Fort Wayne Daisies, meanwhile, were facing the Grand Rapids Chicks. In Kenosha, Rockford won the third game, 8–3, on Snookie Harrell Doyle's two triples and three singles. The next night Rockford sewed up the first round of playoffs with a 5–1 victory behind the pitching of Lois Florreich. With Fort Wayne triumphing over Grand Rapids, the 1950 Shaughnessy saw

Manager	Teams	Manager	Teams
Bill Allington °	Peaches, Daisies	Bert Niehoff *	Blue Sox
Dave Bancroft *	Colleens, Blue Sox, Belles	Marty McManus *	Comets, Blue Sox
Carson Bigbee *	Sallies, Lassies	Leo Murphy *	Belles, Redwings
Max Carey *	Chicks, Daisies	Johnny Rawlings *	Chicks, Redwings, Peaches
Joe Cooper	Belles, Lassies	Leo Schrall	Redwings
Norm Derringer	Belles, Lassies	Mitch Skupien	Chicks, Lassies
Woody English *	Chicks	Eddie Stumpf *	Peaches, Comets
Johnny Gottselig	Belles, Redwings, Comets, Chicks	Bill Wambsganss *	Daisies, Lassies
Chet Grant	Blue Sox, Comets	Karl Winsch °	Blue Sox

the Peaches and the Daisies, the old 1945 rivals, face one another again.

This time around, the Daisies were a powerhouse of a team. Managed by Max Carey, who hadn't piloted a team since he led the 1944 Milwaukee Chicks to victory, Fort Wayne had a collection of sluggers unique in AAGBL history—particularly Betty Weaver Foss, whose .346 average was tops in the league that year. Because Carey and Allington maintained a strong rivalry as managers, Wilma Briggs felt that the two teams "stepped it up" when they met.

Stepping a little faster than the Daisies, the Peaches won the first game, 3–1. The Daisies took a 1–0 lead in the first inning of the second game, but the Peaches scored seven runs in the second inning to win the game, 7–2.

Because of their own skills and Allington's exceptional managing, the Peaches, whether 1945 or 1950 vintage, were tough to beat in every phase of the game. And although fewer fans came to the games, those who did were as Peach-crazy as ever. "You'll never beat the Peaches!" they would yell at the buses bringing rivals into town. At the second game fans took up a collection for catcher Ruth Richard, who had broken her ankle in the last game of the season. Gathering $602, they turned it over to Richard, who would wear a cast for eight more weeks.

Moving on to Fort Wayne—and into miserable mist and rain— the Peaches lost the third game, 7–3. Bolstered by their hometown fans, the strong Daisies also took the fourth game, 5–3, with Maxine Kline on the mound for Fort Wayne and Helen Nicol "Nicky" Fox for Rockford. Betty Foss, Dottie Schroeder, Thelma

Eisen, Wilma Briggs, Evelyn Wawryshyn, and Sally Meier contributed to the Daisy offense.

The fifth game found Rose Gacioch and Dottie Collins facing each other, with Fox relieving Gacioch. After nine innings, the game stood at 2–2. With one out in the top of the tenth, Allington and the Peaches pulled off a bit of daring baseball. Key was hit by a pitch, Kamenshek sacrificed, and Doyle walked. With two outs and runners at first and second, Jackie Kelley hit a ball that ricocheted off Collins's glove, scoring Key and sending Doyle to third. Leading 3–2, the Peaches needed an insurance run. They got it when Doyle on third and Kelley on first pulled a double steal, Doyle scoring and Kelley landing safely on second. The steal provided the winning run, for the Daisies scored one in the bottom of the tenth. With their 4–3 victory, the Peaches held a 3–2 edge in the Shaughnessy Series.

The sixth game was played in Rockford. There, the Peaches fell apart as the Daisies slugged out an 8–0 victory, with Foss hitting an inside-the-park home run over Eleanor Callow's head. On the mound for the Peaches that night, Louise Erickson had no control, while Daisy pitcher Maxine Kline gave up eight hits but kept them scattered.

By this time many of the Peaches who went to college, Dottie Kamenshek among them, were overdue at school. Kammie, in particular, planned to leave Rockford immediately after the seventh game ended. In the final contest she slapped out two singles, a triple, and a homer, driving in five runs and pacing the Peaches to an 11–0 blowout and their fourth championship in eight years of league play.

Pitcher Dolores Lee and Bill Allington,

Rockford Peaches

At the end of the 1952 season, when the Peaches lost the Shaughnessy Series to the South Bend Blue Sox, Bill Allington left the team to manage the Daisies—possibly because of a salary dispute, possibly because he was driven to win and thought he stood a better chance of doing so with the Daisies. Johnny Rawlings, former manager of the Grand Rapids Chicks, took over the Peaches.

In 1954, the AAGBL's last year, the Rockford press ran large photos of the new Peaches at the beginning of the season, but soon coverage dwindled dramatically, along with attendance at games. Sometimes only a hundred fans were scattered throughout the stands. It was the same all around the Midwest, as people turned to new recreational opportunities, bought new cars and drove them on newly constructed expressways to bigger cities, or sat home and watched television.

On June 19, the Rockford Peaches dropped to last place in a five-team league. Even with salaries cut, veterans such as Dottie Ferguson Key and Rose Gacioch continued to play. A few rookies joined the league, sharing with their battle-scarred teammates a belief that nothing could be more wonderful than playing baseball for a living.

By mid-August, coverage of the Peaches was perfunctory, and then it ceased, with no coverage of the playoffs (the Peaches weren't contenders). On September 5, 1954, the final game of the AAGBL was played in Fort Wayne, where the Kalamazoo (Mich.) Lassies upset the Fort Wayne Daisies to win the final Shaughnessy Series. The All-American Girls Baseball League died while people were looking the other way.

Yet the Peaches remain a presence in the town of Rockford today. Fifty-year-olds will talk to you about the games they went to as kids. Thirty-year-olds will tell you of hearing stories about the Peaches and wistfully wishing they could have been there. Ten-year-olds watch *A League of Their Own* and look at their grandmothers and their grandmothers' friends with new-found respect. Today, millions know about the Rockford Peaches.

"The Rockford camaraderie between town and team has a direct, if subtle, bearing on the Peaches' play. As last year's league commissioner Fred Leo explained, 'That team stays pretty consistent. It probably has fewer bad nights than any other on the circuit. Even after a long bus ride, say from Rockford to Grand Rapids, the Peaches hit that field with a lot of hustle. They seem to know what's expected of them, and they don't let their rooters down.'

"Such enthusiasm is not always easy to sustain when the summer heat smothers the Midwest, and the flare-skirted uniform designed by Wrigley artist Otis Shepherd suddenly takes on weight in the airless nights. A hard-working catcher like Ruthie Richard will drop five pounds in a single game and be semi-sobbing with exhaustion at the end of a tough doubleheader. Then the glamour of the game seems remote, and the disciplined routines of day-by-day pro ball become abrasive.

"'It's a job,' explained Allington, sagely. 'When that schedule turns into a jail sentence, you know where your ballplayers are and who your real competitors are.'"

—Carl L. Biemiller, *Holiday* magazine, June 1952

Jean Faut

IN SEVEN YEARS OF OVERHAND PITCHING, TWO PERFECT games were pitched in the All-American Girls Baseball League—and Jean Faut of the South Bend Blue Sox hurled them both. "She had great strength," says catcher Shirley Stovroff, "and she was very smart. She had a mixture of pitches—fastball, curve, drop, slowball—and she had excellent control." The league's leading hitter, Dottie Kamenshek, evaluates Faut this way: "She put them all just where she wanted." Pitching overhand was never foreign to the Blue Sox ace. She grew up playing hardball, and when the league switched to overhand, Jean was like a fish in water, moving effortlessly through the environment.

Few pitchers were able to make a successful transition from underhand to overhand. Among those who did were Dottie Wiltse Collins, Joanne Winter, and Helen Nicol Fox. Those who couldn't went back to softball or, like Connie Wisniewski, converted to another position. By 1948, when the league went overhand, softball had all but obliterated baseball as a sport for women, and ironically the AAGBL, which started out by capitalizing on the softball craze, found as it moved toward the more exciting and exacting game of baseball that pitchers were suddenly difficult

AAGBL PLAYER OF THE YEAR AWARD

	Player	Team
1945	Connie Wisniewski	Grand Rapids Chicks
1946	Sophie Kurys	Racine Belles
1947	Doris Sams	Muskegon Lassies
1948	Audrey Wagner	Kenosha Comets
1949	Doris Sams	Muskegon Lassies
1950	Alma Ziegler	Grand Rapids Chicks
1951	Jean Faut	South Bend Blue Sox
1952	Betty Foss	Fort Wayne Daisies
1953	Jean Faut	South Bend Blue Sox
1954	Joanne Weaver	Fort Wayne Daisies

Jean Faut, South Bend Blue Sox

to find. In desperation league managers began to convert their hardest-throwing outfielders (who naturally throw overhand) into pitchers.

These converted outfielders learned about pitching from their managers, from watching their teammates, and from being on the mound themselves. Their knowledge was only as deep as their league pitching experience. Jean Faut's was not. "I had more experience than most of the girls in the AAGBL," she contends. "I came into the league with a fastball, a sharp curve, screwball, drop and change—and a lot of deviations from these basic pitches." Born January 17, 1925, in East Greenville, Pennsylvania, Jean grew up two blocks away from the practice field of a semipro baseball team. She hung around the field and yearned to play, and by the time she was thirteen the players had taught her how to pitch. Faut learned so well that when she was still in high school she pitched several exhibition games for the semipro Buck-Montgomery League, an experience she describes as "a great thrill."

In 1946 a scout from Allentown, Pennsylvania, offered the five-foot-four, 137-pound young ballplayer a chance to attend AAGBL spring training in Pascagoula, Mississippi. "The rookies went in first," she remembers. "All the representatives were there from the cities, the board of directors. They chose who they wanted." After finishing fifth out of six teams in 1945 with a 40–60 record, the South Bend Blue Sox would have been among the first to select players. Board Director Harold Dailey, who had smarted so badly from losing Rose Gacioch to Rockford in 1945, wrote of the 1946 tryouts, "We got Wirth and Faut out of the deal."

The Blue Sox started Senaida "Shoo Shoo" Wirth as shortstop

and Jean Faut as third baseman. "I had a strong arm," she says, "so third was a natural spot." Late in her rookie season, the league permitted some sidearm pitching and manager Chet Grant asked Faut to take the mound. Although she didn't like to pitch sidearm because "it's not very good for your arm, almost like throwing a screwball," she started twelve games, winning eight and losing three. The league went to overhand in 1948. "I was ready then," she states. "I was home free."

When Jean Faut moved to South Bend, Karl Winsch followed her there. A pitcher in the Philadelphia Phillies organization, Winsch was called up to the majors in 1946 along with his room-mate Del Ennis, who flourished there. But Winsch sustained an injury in spring training that ended his career. When that happened, he moved to South Bend and in 1947 he and Jean were married. In that year, Chet Grant sent his sophomore to the mound in forty-four games, and she posted a 19–13 record with a 1.15 ERA. By midseason, Jean was pregnant; she gave birth to her first child in March 1948. Writing about the Blue Sox 1948 season, Harold Dailey opined that "Faut was not in condition until July owing to the drag on her by pregnancy." Starting thirty-four games, she compiled a 16–11 record.

Faut turned twenty-four years old before the 1949 season began. "I started to mature," she reflects. "You get better, your control gets better. You work on new pitches." The overhand ace was now in her element. In 1949 she started thirty-four games and racked up a 24–8 record and a 1.10 ERA.

Unlike Lois Florreich, another great hurler of the overhand era, Faut didn't have intimidating speed. Outstanding hitters such as

Dottie Kamenshek rank Faut as the best pitcher of the league's overhand days despite her lack of velocity, recognizing that what matters is whether the pitcher gets the batter out, not the speed of the ball as it crosses the plate. Yet many hitters' perception of greatness is thrown off by speed: they rank the pitcher who gets them out on a blazing fastball higher than the one who gets them out on an adequate fastball, or on a combination of pitches. Umpires, too, were baffled by Faut's success. One of the umpires even stepped into the batter's box during practice and bragged, "I can hit you." So Faut whiffed him. "Afterward, he still didn't understand why he couldn't hit me." Even her own manager, Davy Bancroft, said he just didn't understand why batters couldn't hit her.

"My biggest asset was control," Faut explains. "I have very strong wrists and could do things with the ball. I got that way splitting wood by the hour when I was a kid." Her variety of pitches also helped. "I had a good curveball and could throw it overhand, three-quarters, or sidearm. If overhand, it went straight down. I threw a screwball, like a slider, but not often. And a fastball. I could throw them with different speeds." And if, as they say in the majors, 90 percent of pitching is mental, Jean Faut had that, too. "Part of my success was that in my mind I could record the pitches and the order of pitches I threw to each girl, so they never saw the same thing twice. I was a mathematical whiz in school. They'd never know what was coming, so they'd start guessing. When batters start guessing, they're never right."

Some analysts of the All-American Girls Baseball League say that the reason batting averages went up so dramatically in the last third of the league's existence was that there were few really good overhand pitchers. Faut disagrees, naming Lois Florreich, Maxine Kline, and Millie Earp as great overhand hurlers. She should know, for in addition to 35–45 pitching appearances a year, Jean often played an additional forty games at third base, where the Blue Sox counted on her fielding and hitting. Faut believes that the hitters coming into the AAGBL in the 1950s were strong athletes who mastered baseball hitting. She points to the Weaver sisters in particular: "Betty Foss would run the bases and the dirt would fly up. One time I was pitching and Betty Foss hit the ball straight at me. It came so straight and fast I couldn't see the spin, couldn't react. I saw the seam and then it hit me in the stomach, there wasn't even time to get my glove up. When I undressed, I saw the stitch marks on my stomach."

Strong hitters or not, Jean could handle them. On July 21, 1951, she pitched a perfect game in Rockford against the Peaches, retiring twenty-seven batters in a row. Dottie Kamen-shek, who prided herself on not striking out, whiffed twice that night. It was, says Kammie, "the best game I've ever seen pitched. It was just perfect. Overpowering." The next morning, the *South Bend Tribune* reported that "Jean Faut, a sturdy gal with a lot of heart, a fast ball that hops, and a curve that breaks off like a country road, pitched a perfect no-hit, no-run game to subdue the Rockford Peaches, 2–0, at Playland Park Saturday night. . . . The chances of a no-hit game were never mentioned in the Blue Sox dugout during the game, according to baseball superstition, but the crowd of 1,490 were fully aware that baseball history was in the making." Whiffing eleven of the twenty-seven batters, the Sox

1951 and 1953 AAGBL Player of the Year, Jean Faut

hurler got behind the count on only two. "She threw three balls to Eleanor Callow in the fifth and then fanned her. One other time she threw three balls, then two strikes, and the batter grounded out."

Faut's 1951 pitching record was 15–7 with a 1.33 ERA. She was chosen Player of the Year and helped lead the Blue Sox to their first Shaughnessy Series victory. In 1952 she went 20–2 (a .909 winning percentage), posted a 0.93 ERA, and once again helped lead her team to a series victory, batting in the cleanup position. With the playoff series tied, she hurled the deciding game against the Peaches, hitting two booming triples for extra measure. In 1953 she pitched her second perfect game, this one against the Kalamazoo Lassies on September 3. That year she was again elected Player of the Year, only the second person in league history to receive the award twice (the other was Doris Sams).

In major league ball, Hall-of-Famer Christy Mathewson

South Bend Blue Sox, 1952: Jean Faut, far left; Karl Winsch, manager

compiled a .665 winning record and a 2.13 lifetime ERA, while latter-day greats such as Sandy Koufax (.655 and 2.76), Bob Gibson (.591 and 2.91), and Tom Seaver (.603 and 2.86) had somewhat lower winning percentages and higher ERAs. Jean Faut's career statistics are 140 wins and 64 losses—a .686 winning percentage and a 1.23 ERA. Of all her accomplishments, she is proudest of her ERA, because "that's the most important statistic of a pitcher."

Although Faut was a real team player, her life on the Blue Sox was that of a loner. It wasn't just that Jean was married and therefore didn't room with another player or take part in their pregame or postgame activities. And it wasn't just that she was raising a child. In 1951, Karl Winsch became manager of the South Bend Blue Sox, a job he held until the league folded. Under Winsch, the Blue Sox won their only two championships, but there was tremendous dissension on the team. Groups of players wouldn't talk to the manager, and then they wouldn't talk to Jean. Winsch wouldn't talk to Jean, either. "Neither side communicated with me," she says. "It was a big squabble." At the end of the 1953 season, she retired from baseball at the age of twenty-eight because it was just too rough being married to the manager.

"I suffered because I wasn't playing," she remembers. At first, she'd go to the games and sit in the stands, but that would make her miserable because she wasn't playing. So, "to fill the void I went to the bowling center." Jean became such a good bowler that in 1960 she turned pro, retiring from that status in 1988. Today she bowls with the senior women's tour. Her highest game to date is a 299, just short of perfect.

Faut, hurler of two perfect games

In 1946, the same year that Jean Faut attended the league try-outs, another Pennsylvania woman went to spring training in Pascagoula. For nine years, Ruth Williams played for the South Bend Blue Sox and then the Kalamazoo Lassies. She'll always remember one game. "Jeannie Faut beat me in sixteen innings, one to nothing, back in 1952," says Williams. "She was pitching for the Blue Sox, I was with the Lassies. I had pitched forty consecutive shutout innings, then I got tied up with Jeannie. She was the best player in the league. She doubled off me in the sixteenth, moved to third on a bunt, and scored on a sacrifice fly. Figured it would be Jeannie that would end my streak." It figured because Jean Faut was to pitching what Dottie Kamenshek was to hitting and Sophie Kurys was to base stealing—without peer.

BASEBALL AND MOTHERHOOD

Toward the end of Jean Faut's AAGBL career, when her son Larry was four or five years old, "he traveled with the team one year [and] wore a little uniform." In Rockford one night, "The managers and umps were meeting at home plate and Larry went out there and ran the bases. I don't know, but I think somebody put him up to it. The fans applauded."

Faut wasn't the only AAGBLer who was a mother. Helen Callaghan, who was married to Robert Candaele, nearly lost her life one night in 1946 when she stepped up to bat and experienced excruciating abdominal pain, so bad that the team called a doctor out of the stands. Although the doctor declared there was nothing wrong, Helen had to be rushed to the hospital, where a tubal pregnancy was correctly diagnosed. Because the hospital couldn't reach Robert Candaele, Helen's sister and teammate, Margaret Callaghan, had to give permission to operate.

The next year Helen gave birth to her first son, Rick. She played one more year of baseball after that, but came to feel the game "just got to be a job after a while. And I just wanted to take care of my family." So she quit the All-American Girls Baseball League and raised five children.

Olive Bend Little was married to George Little before she started to play for the Rockford Peaches in 1943, posting a 21–15 record her rookie year. She took the next year off to have their first child, daughter Bobbie. When Little returned to the Peaches in 1945, she was honored with an "Olive Little Night" and commented that the event was so wonderful it made her feel like having another baby. In 1945 she posted a 22–11 record and helped the Peaches win their first championship. After playing the 1946 season, she retired from the league to raise a family.

Dottie Wiltse joined the league in 1944 and met Harvey Collins the next year, when he asked her out after seeing her pitch and win both ends of a doubleheader. Eventually they married, and she continued to pitch as Dottie Collins. In 1948, Dottie was pregnant before the season began, but only she and Harvey,

her doctor, and Daisy manager Dick Bass knew it.

Both Collins and her doctor agreed that she was strong enough and healthy enough to pitch. Her doctor believed that a physically active person shouldn't quit athletics overnight just because she was pregnant. Dick Bass, however, "was a nervous wreck" every time Dottie pitched and would always ask her when she was going to quit.

When she was six months pregnant, Collins pitched the first game of a Sunday doubleheader and knew it was time. "Dick," she said to her manager, "I quit."

"Thank god," Bass responded.

Isabel Alvarez

FOR MORE THAN A CENTURY, *PELOTA DE BÉISBOL* HAS been a passion in Cuba. Introduced to the island by Cuban students and American sailors, the game swept Cuba in the latter part of the nineteenth century. By 1879, championship series games were being played, and by 1910, American major league teams were traveling to the island for exhibition games against locals. In 1914, Adolfo Luque, "The Pride of Havana," entered the major leagues as a pitcher, spending the better part of his twenty-one-year, 194-win career with Cincinnati.

During the 1940s, no fewer than twenty-two Cubans entered the U.S. major leagues, while back home independently wealthy distillery owner Rafael de Leon formed a baseball league modeled on the All-American Girls Baseball League. "Rafael de Leon did the same for Cuba that [Max] Carey did for the United States," says Isabel Alvarez. "They had the same vision." Calling his group *Estrellas Cubanas* ("Cuban Stars") and outfitting them in the AAGBL-style tunic, de Leon recruited the best ballplayers among island women.

When she was growing up in Cuba, says Isabel Alvarez, a black Cuban neighbor, an ex-ballplayer, taught her "all about baseball."

When de Leon's league was formed, Isabel's mother encouraged her to play, took her to practice, and paved the way for her to go to the United States. Although her brother Antonio also played ball, it was young Isabel who took the U.S. baseball road and entered a different kind of life. Like many a Latin American player, she came to a land that offered her material goods but cultural loneliness.

Born October 31, 1933, Isabel was quite young at the time she joined the *Estrellas Cubanas*, probably twelve or thirteen. "Rafael de Leon built a park and house for the women ballplayers so [we] could train. He fed us and everything," she recalls. "We ballplayers were very poor. We enjoyed going [to his estate] for the weekend." De Leon must have seen great talent in the girl who quit school after the sixth grade. "He bought me my own glove and he said, 'Isabelita, you're going to be the next girl to go to the United States, but we have to wait until you're fifteen.'"

Isabel Alvarez, age fourteen, at bat in Venezuela

Alvarez, age sixteen, on tour with AAGBL
Colleens

The first Cuban woman to play baseball in the United States was nineteen-year-old Eulalia Gonzales, who played for the Racine Belles a short time in 1947 before homesickness made her quit. The next *Cubanas* to arrive came in 1949: Isabel Alvarez, Ysora del Castillo, Mirtha Marrero, and Migdalia Perez. Just as Rafael de Leon had come to realize it was wiser to send a group of young players rather than just one, the AAGBL had come to recognize the necessity of establishing some kind of minor-league system to train young ballplayers. Improvising, the AAGBL sent a busload of young ballplayers on the road. Wearing the uniforms of the defunct Springfield Sallies and Chicago Colleens, two teams of women traveled thousands of miles a summer, playing ball in different towns every night. Fifteen-year-old pitcher Alvarez and first baseman Castillo played for the Colleens, pitchers Marrero and Perez for the Sallies.

For two seasons, Alvarez traveled with the hopefuls. Mitch Skupien, who would later become an AAGBL manager, reported to the board of directors in 1950: "Isabel Alvarez—Has a beautiful motion but throws a soft pitch. Converted from sidearm to overhand in midseason and started to show improvement, but still think not ready. Suggest tour another year. Shows promise for future."

There would not be another tour: by 1951 the management of the AAGBL had changed hands, entering its third and final phase. After the two-year guidance of Philip K. Wrigley and the six-year administration of Arthur Meyerhoff, the disgruntled franchise owners went independent, renaming their organization the American Girls Baseball League. Seeking to economize, they cut publicity immediately and training soon after. The traveling bus that had carried Alvarez and twenty-nine others was abandoned, and the players were either let go or moved up. Alvarez went to the Fort Wayne Daisies.

She remembers the two years of road trips as wonderful. "I wasn't alone," she says. "I liked those years. We rode the bus together." The *Cubanas* had one another to talk baseball with and

RACIAL INTEGRATION

In 1947 the All-American Girls Baseball League held spring training in Havana, Cuba, playing games to crowds larger than those that went to see Jackie Robinson and the Brooklyn Dodgers, who were also training there. The Dodgers were in Cuba because they believed it wasn't possible to train a racially integrated team in the U.S. South without meeting violent racist opposition.

The time and the place were perfect for the AAGBL to integrate, but the men who ran the league never chose to do so. Although they did address the question at a business meeting during the 1950s, they let it pass unanswered.

Two factors worked against racial integration of the league. One was certainly that the Negro Leagues, from which the

majors drew the talented black players of the late 1940s and early 1950s, were, like the majors, open only to men—at least until the early 1950s, when three women were signed to play. Black women, like white women, were given softball as a substitute for the real thing. By the late 1940s, unless an organization was looking very hard, finding black female baseball players was not easy. Yet black women could have been recruited from softball players, just as white women were. The Admiral Music Maids of the National Girls Baseball League (a softball league, despite its name) in Chicago did recruit Betty Chapman in 1951, and former AAGBLers such as Joanne Winter were among her teammates.

A second factor that prevented the

AAGBL board of directors from seeking racial integration was that from the league's inception, the men in charge believed that only a certain kind of woman should be recruited—one who met society's standards of "feminine beauty." For these men, it was inconceivable that a woman without makeup could be beautiful or feminine. And so they required that baseball players take the field wearing lipstick and nail polish. Social mores of the time excluded black women from the standards of "feminine beauty." In order to recruit black women to the league, the AAGBL directors would have had to overcome both racism and sexism. That men who made women play baseball in short skirts couldn't do so should come as no surprise.

helped each other learn English. "On the tour, it was beautiful because we were all together on the bus and we were all the same age. The managers and coaches were wonderful. They were like family."

In Fort Wayne, with no fellow Cubans, things were different. "I was alone in Fort Wayne," Alvarez remembers painfully. "Sometimes when you can't communicate, you feel maybe [others] don't want you around. Everyone has a clique, they run around in groups." Boarding with a family in Fort Wayne, Isabel was on her own, without even a roommate—something neither Wrigley nor Meyerhoff would have allowed. "On the bus I was with them and had a roommate on tour. After, I had no roommate to pick. Many would say, 'I don't know her too well.'

"One night at the hotel, I was all alone on a Sunday. There was

The traveling Colleens: Alvarez, front row, second from right

no game. In the morning, I'd get up and wouldn't know what to do with myself. I heard a railroad train, *oooooooooo,* a sad sound. Now when I hear a train like that, I always come back to that night when I stayed in the room alone."

During the off-season, the southpaw with the soft pitch returned to Cuba. There her mother made her write letters to one or two friends in the league. For Isabel, who found writing itself an intimidating process and who was not fluent in English, it was a difficult job as she picked words out of a dictionary one by one. It became clear to Alvarez that her mother wanted her to play baseball in the United States and stay there because "then she wouldn't have to worry about me. Then the U.S. was tops economically." No matter how intense the loneliness, she had to stick it out. "I had a job to do," she explains. "I wasn't allowed to say, 'Ma, I'm homesick.' I had to do my job and forget about Cuba."

Very young and very shy, Alvarez felt she couldn't make friends as easily as outgoing Mirtha Marrero. The American players seemed to relate better to somebody like Cuban-born Gloria Ruiz, who allowed them to dye her hair blond. "I was just a child," says Alvarez. "I felt I could have done better. [But] my culture is so different."

In 1951 Alvarez appeared in thirteen games for the Fort Wayne Daisies. Pitching thirty-nine innings, she earned two wins and no losses. Traded a lot, she played for the Kalamazoo Lassies, the Grand Rapids Chicks, and the Battle Creek Belles before ending up with the Daisies again in 1954. "Fair" is how she rates herself as a pitcher. "I was not a superstar, I just did my job." She assesses the other *Cubanas* in the same way: "We did our job, but we

Isabel Alvarez, at right

didn't become great. I could have been better if I'd had more self-confidence, but I stayed back." For her, the language barrier was almost insurmountable and affected her ability to develop as a pitcher. The players who spoke English to one another had a tremendous advantage. "They could *talk* about baseball to each other," says Isabel, adding that they could develop as players by discussing their actions. She could not. "If you can't communicate, you stand still."

The race is not always to the swift nor assimilation to the popular. Gloria Ruiz of the dyed blond hair returned to Cuba, as did the popular Mirtha Marrero. Isabel Alvarez stayed. In Fort Wayne she found friends in the world outside baseball. "This is why I stayed here. It was my salvation." Her friends took her to English classes and helped her study for the citizenship papers she received in 1959. Not long after, she began working at an electronics plant.

Alvarez made it through the intense loneliness of her AAGBL years because she came to accept her mother's goals for her and because a few teammates and manager Bill Allington did help her walk the one-way street of assimilation. "He talked to me," she says of Allington. "He told me things [and] was really trying to help me. And he did, he helped me be better." Although she considers herself just a "fair" player, Allington must have seen more than that in the young lefty— he asked her to tour with his barnstorming team after the league's demise. Isabel would have loved to go but didn't "because of my work. I needed my job and couldn't afford to give it up."

Today the passing of time, growing pride on Alvarez's part, and perhaps less ethnocentrism on the part of others have brought the women of the All-American Girls Baseball League closer together. Their small group of fewer than six hundred experienced something that set them apart from others of their generation. "Now when we have reunions," says Alvarez, "it's beautiful."

OTHER *CUBANAS*

Like Isabel Alvarez, Ysora Castillo grew up playing baseball in Cuba, but unlike Alvarez she was taught the game by her father. Castillo toured Latin America with one of the several combined *Cubanas-Americanas* teams during the late 1940s, and when the AAGBL offered her a contract in 1949, the seventeen-year-old first baseman received her family's permission to go.

In the United States, Castillo played infield for the Kalamazoo Lassies. "I was always talking out there," she remembers. "But I couldn't speak English so nobody knew what I was saying." When she chattered, *"Arriba chica!,"* the players thought she was saying "Chico," so that's what they called her: Chico. "Nobody knew my real name," says Ysora.

Adelina Garcia grew up playing baseball every day with her seven brothers and sisters and other neighborhood children. When the Havana newspapers announced that the All-American Girls Baseball League would be in town to hold tryouts, Garcia decided to attend. "When my parents found out that I was leaving home to join the team, they had a fit," she said. "It was my neighbors, who knew how hard it was for us to make ends meet, who finally convinced [them] to give me permission to go." Neighbors then took up a collection to buy Adelina a suit and her first pair of leather shoes so she could attend the training camp.

Watching Garcia throw during infield practice, an American manager immediately converted her to a pitcher. Soon she got the nickname *Velocidad García* ("Speedy García") for her fastball.

Offered a contract to tour with the American and Cuban teams in Latin America, she signed it. While touring, she was taught how to throw a curveball, as was teammate Mirtha Marrero.

In 1949 the AAGBL offered Mirtha Marrero and Isabel Alvarez contracts to come to the United States, but Adelina Garcia wasn't offered one. After the Cuban revolution she served as an official in a hotel workers' union. Married and the mother of two daughters, she recounted her baseball days in 1982, when, in preparation for the Central American Games to be held in Cuba that year, the Cuban press began to report on the history of women's softball and discovered (as have American newspapers) that women played baseball long before they played softball.

Lois Youngen

Catcher Lois Youngen, Fort Wayne Daisies

IN THE SPRING OF 1951, HIGH SCHOOL SENIOR LOIS YOUNGEN of Ragersville, Ohio, embarked on a two-week trip with her class. The sixteen students and their teacher-chaperone took the train to Washington, D.C. "All the steel mills were going at that time," remembers Lois. "At night, you could see the glow from the Bessemer furnaces as we passed through Youngstown and Pittsburgh. It was marvelous." After one week in D.C., fifteen of the seniors continued on to New York City. Lois stayed behind. This five-foot-four, 120-pound young lady, raised by well-educated, middle-class parents, had received an invitation to attend the spring tryouts of the AAGBL in Alexandria, Virginia, where the Battle Creek Belles and the Fort Wayne Daisies were training. If all went as Youngen hoped it would, she would earn the hottest, sweatiest, dirtiest baseball job of all—she would become a catcher.

The daughter of two educators (her mother was a teacher and her father a principal and later a superintendent of schools), Lois grew up well-read and with a passion for baseball. Her father, who had been a star of the Kent State University baseball team and a semipro pitcher, played catch with her regularly, and her two uncles were Ragersville town ballplayers—both had played on the Weiss All-Stars, and one of them had been Alta Weiss's catcher. "When I grew up, if I wanted to play baseball with the boys, they made me be the catcher," says Youngen. Her attitude became that of a catcher. "I was never afraid. Give me the ball—I can do it." So she took the position that faces the other way and the AAGBL took her, signing her to the Fort Wayne Daisies.

When spring training was over, she traveled with the Daisies and Belles for their exhibition games, including one in Griffith Stadium, home of the Washington Senators. Lois had her picture taken with Senators' owner Clark Griffith, a former major league pitcher, and recalls the excitement of being on a major league field. "I can remember standing in the batter's box and saying, 'Joe DiMaggio stood here.' I walked to the other side and said, 'Ted Williams stood here.' It was a great thrill."

After the spring tour, she returned to Ohio to graduate, reporting to the Daisies in June 1951. There were still eight teams in the AAGBL at that time, and Fort Wayne, managed by Max Carey, looked like a winner with awesome Betty Foss and her young sister, Jo "The Jolter" Weaver, Wilma Briggs, base-stealing veteran Tiby Eisen, and others. Youngen didn't expect to play much as a rookie, and she didn't. "I went in to run the bases a lot in the eighth and ninth innings." Occasionally she got to catch the last couple of innings. At the end of the season, "they shipped me off to play with the Comets for the last two or three weeks, to give me more experience."

By 1952 the league had shrunk to six teams, resulting in much shifting around of players. Youngen was still with the Daisies, but Max Carey left and was replaced by Jimmie Foxx. She remembers that the famous major league slugger, nicknamed Double X and

The Beast in the bigs, was gentle and reticent, a manager who treated all his players with respect and who never worshiped the spotlight. "We tried to get him to take batting practice once in a while, but he was reluctant," says Lois. "Perhaps three or four times he did it at home, not on the road. We'd finally talk him into it and he'd just plummet it over the fence. It was maybe 260 feet to center, then there was a field beyond that, then a four-lane highway. Foxx hit the highway. He'd only hit four or five, but when he connected, it was long gone.

"I adored him," confesses Youngen, who got her manager's autograph at the end of the season. "He wasn't outgoing, and he was very low-key. He'd say, 'Let's go get the job done.'" Today she wishes she hadn't been so shy and had talked to Foxx more often, to learn more about baseball.

Just playing in the league, though, and applying native intelligence to the situation, Lois Youngen learned plenty. Her "tools of ignorance," as the catcher's gear is called, were provided by the AAGBL: a chest protector that "was always too large," shinguards that came over the knees, and a mask that wasn't heavy-duty— more like a softball mask. "I got hit on the mask a couple of times," she says. "Once it hurt my jaw so badly I couldn't even eat." Like the other players, the catcher provided her own glove.

Behind the plate Youngen called the game, using the time-honored signals: one finger for a fastball, two for the curve, three for a changeup, a fist for the pitchout. "Some threw a slider," she explains, "a minicurve, so to speak, but we had no signal for a slider." To protect the signals from the opposing coach on third, the catcher let her glove hang over her bare hand, blocking his view.

One of the real dangers of the catcher's job is to that bare hand, particularly the fingers. Former major league umpire Ron Luciano once said of catchers, "They are the only athletes I know who can stick their hands out straight and point behind them." A catcher must stop the ball—with the free hand if she can't stop it with the glove hand. When a ball comes in where the catcher doesn't expect it, on a wild pitch or misunderstood call, it can bruise or break a finger. "Today the free hand goes behind your back," Youngen explains. "We were taught to hold our fingers curled and hold them loosely. I held mine behind my glove. But even though my catcher's glove was very small, not half of the size of a major league outfielder's glove, my fingers were never injured. You'd never know I caught."

But more and more she did, and just by being catcher was required to act a veteran. Alongside the tough physical job, there's the psychological work. "It's important for a catcher to know if her pitcher has the stuff going into the game," she says, and even though she was young herself, a twenty-year-old college student by 1953, she played the game professionally. If a young

Fort Wayne Daisies, 1952: Lois Youngen, front center; Jimmie Foxx, manager

pitcher needed calming down, Lois walked out to the mound to do the job. "Dolly Vanderlip was young and she got nervous and could get wild. So I'd go out and say, 'Hey, you've done this ten thousand times before. You've been successful at it. Just put it in my glove.'"

Unlike their counterparts in the majors, AAGBL catchers seldom razzed the batter. "I didn't do that too much, and I can't remember any who did," Youngen says. "I talked more to our pitcher than to the batter." Chattering to her pitcher, Lois would repeat phrases such as "Make a hitter out of her" and throw in an occasional "Hummm, baby." Facing forward, the catcher would never turn to the umpire. "You never *look* at the ump," she explains. But she would talk to the man behind her. "Come on, ump. Open up!" she would lament when she thought the man in blue had too narrow a strike zone. Sometimes the umpires would talk back. "I've got six starving children and a wife who wants a divorce," one would reply.

In 1953, Lois Youngen was with the South Bend Blue Sox, sharing plate duties with catcher Mary Baumgartner and playing left field. In the AAGBL, with its basic-baseball hit-and-run style of play, runners frequently slid into home. "It happened all the time. You were expected to block the plate whether you had the ball or not. It didn't matter if you got knocked flat on your back— you were expected to tag the runner." Youngen was knocked flat on her back more than once, but she was never intimidated by it. "I was always eager to get the ball," she says. "And I was confident I could catch anything anybody threw at me."

The following year, the AAGBL was down to five teams and

Youngen was back with the Fort Wayne Daisies. At midseason, the ten-inch league ball was replaced with a regulation baseball. "It made a tremendous difference to me," she remembers. "The smaller ball was easier to get a grip on and throw." The smaller ball could also be hit further, and like her teammates, Lois began smacking the regulation baseball all over the field, driving in three runs with a triple here, one run with a single there, and raising her batting average to .284. Part of the reason for her improved average, she believes, was that she played more and got to see the ball more. Had the league had more batting practice, Youngen feels she could have been a .300 hitter. But with cutbacks on managers' salaries and players' pay, there was less and less batting practice. And travel time had always cut into practice time.

"I was never a star catcher," she maintains. "I was a yeoman middle-of-the-road ballplayer." Maybe. Or maybe, as former major league catcher Bob Boone said of catching, "If you're doing a quality job, you should be almost anonymous." It's likely that's the kind of catcher Youngen was: she did her job so well—signaled the number of outs to the team, calmed her pitcher, called the pitches, threw down to first, second, and third, blocked the plate and held on to the ball—nobody knew she was there.

Yet yeoman Youngen did something spectacular—something that testifies to how good the average AAGBL player was. On September 3, 1953, Jean Faut of the South Bend Blue Sox pitched the second perfect game in league overhand history. In Kalamazoo, twenty-seven Lassies faced Faut and went down in order as the Blue Sox won, 7–0. The yeoman catcher was Lois Youngen.

Dr. Lois Youngen, Head of Physical Activity and Recreational Services, University of Oregon

In 1955, the first season after the All-American Girls Baseball League came to an end, Bill Allington formed a women's team called Allington's All-Stars. Lois Youngen toured with the team that first year. Wearing uniforms almost identical to those of the AAGBL, the small band of ballplayers barnstormed the U.S. in a bus, challenging men's town and semipro teams to games much as the Bloomer Girls had done from 1892 to 1934.

Unlike the Bloomer Girls, Allington's All-Stars carried no male players. Either at Allington's urging or that of the teams they were playing, the All-Stars adopted the policy of exchanging batteries. This meant that Youngen and her batterymate played for the men against the women, while the male catcher and pitcher played for the women against the men. The logic behind it was that a man would be pitching to men and a woman to women, and this would even the odds and lessen the chance of injury. Any male runner sliding home would encounter a male catcher; any woman runner sliding home would encounter a female catcher. Of course, this would occur only seven-

ninths of the time—the female catcher and pitcher still had to bat for the men's team, and vice-versa. Youngen remembers that it was tough facing male pitchers, many of whom would throw her nothing but brushback pitches. "I spent a lot of time picking myself up off the dirt," she says. In those days, the players didn't have batting helmets. "It boggles my mind now," she shudders. "I'm surprised I got out of the tour alive."

Although the All-Stars toured again in 1956 and 1957, Youngen did not. In 1955 she graduated from Kent State University with a B.S. in Physical Education and in 1957 she received a graduate degree from Michigan State University. She became an assistant professor in women's physical education at the University of Oregon, Eugene, and after a leave to earn her Ph.D. from Ohio State University in 1971, she returned to Oregon and was appointed Acting Graduate Coordinator for the Department of Physical Education and Human Movement Studies. Today she is head of the university's Physical Activity and Recreational Services.

Part 4

THE
MODERN
YEARS

FROM THE MOMENT WOMEN FIRST PLAYED THE GAME for pay up to the midpoint of the twentieth century, women's endeavors in baseball moved forward along three different paths: sexually integrated baseball teams such as the Bloomer Girls; individuals who joined men's teams, as in the case of Alta Weiss and Jackie Mitchell; and the sexually segregated teams of the All-American Girls Baseball League.

Each path eventually reached an impasse, but for different reasons. Because they were funded by promoters who weren't wealthy, the bloomer teams folded during the Great Depression, when it became impossible to finance such teams. The efforts of individual women to enter organized baseball also ended during the 1930s, when Commissioner Kenesaw Mountain Landis erected a police roadblock by decreeing that the game was too strenuous for women. And the path of sexual segregation reached a dead end when television turned most fans into couch potatoes, and every radio commercial, magazine ad, and television show worked to persuade women that their place was in the home.

During the modern years, each forgotten path has been rediscovered.

In 1984, Bob Hope of the Atlanta Braves organization announced that he would field an all-women's team, the Sun Sox, and apply for a Class A minor league franchise. He soon found that he could not immediately field nineteen women qualified to play Class A ball, so he ended up with a sexually integrated baseball team.

Toni Stone and Julie Croteau both played on otherwise all-men's teams—Stone on the Indianapolis Clowns of the Negro

Leagues and Croteau on the St. Mary's College Seahawks, an NCAA Division III team. Female umpires, too, stepped onto the diamond in isolated cases. Bernice Gera, Christine Wren, and Pam Postema each took this route.

Anybody wishing to start an entire women's professional baseball league today would find the expense almost prohibitive. After Penny Marshall's *A League of Their Own* opened to favorable reviews and much publicity, there was talk that some entrepreneur or promoter would start an all-female professional baseball league modeled on the AAGBL, but to date nobody has.

One difference between the modern years and the previous periods is that the social struggles of the 1960s marched down the highways in the interim, erecting new road signs such as the Civil Rights Act of 1964. Bernice Gera became an umpire in organized baseball only after the courts determined that her civil rights had been violated.

Today the officials of organized baseball speak different words with different intonations than did Commissioner Landis. They talk about wanting "minorities" in baseball—and when prodded or reminded that women are not among "minorities," they add that they want women, too. Certainly the business end of baseball has opened up opportunities for many skilled and talented women, but the playing field remains as off-limits as ever. The words are different, the results the same. Organized baseball heads into the twenty-first century determined to keep the field of dreams as a male privilege.

Today women are different, too: taller, stronger, and less willing to take no for an answer. New studies of human physiology and new training methods have produced stronger female athletes than ever before. Olympic medalists such as Jackie Joyner-Kersey show the potential women have. Although even the greatest female athlete will have less muscle mass (and therefore less speed and strength) than the greatest male athlete, baseball players are not chosen by heft. Little League, American Legion, college ball, and the minors are not body-building gymnasiums, but institutions that teach glove work, follow-through, and heads-up baseball.

With the hard-won victory that finally opened the Little League to girls in 1974, thousands of girls a year have shown their interest in the nation's pastime. With its distances, complexities, speed, and the glory of its history, baseball appeals to them and for some becomes a passion. Just as 75 percent of today's major-leaguers have come from the ranks of Little League, so tomorrow's female baseball players will start there and follow the path through Pony League, Babe Ruth League, high school and college ball. The road into the minor leagues is well marked, but as the history of the modern years reveals, traveling it will be rough indeed.

Toni Stone

THE WORD *FIRST* MEANS LITTLE TO MARCENIA LYLE ALBERGA, the word *play* everything—she is far prouder of the fact that she played professional baseball than that she was the first woman to do so in a men's league. That the Negro League in which she played was on its way to extinction hints that the motives of those who hired her weren't necessarily pure, and had there been a commissioner of the Negro Leagues it's possible he would have rescinded her contract just as major league commissioner Kenesaw Mountain Landis voided Jackie Mitchell's. But there was no such commissioner, and what matters for Alberga is that she played the game.

Marcenia Lyle was born in 1921, one of four children of a black Catholic family that moved from the South to St. Paul, Minnesota. Her father had run away from home to become a barber, and her mother was a beautician. Neither parent could understand why their daughter was attracted to baseball. "They would have stopped me if they could," she remembers, "but there was nothing they could do about it." There was nothing her siblings could do about it, either. When Wheaties cereal sponsored

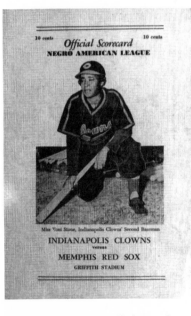

Toni Stone on program of Indianapolis Clowns, 1953

baseball clubs that kids could join by collecting the requisite number of box tops, Marcenia forced one of her sisters, who liked neither baseball nor Wheaties, to eat the cereal every day until the box-top goal was achieved.

Encouraged to play ball by those who recognized her talents, the young girl joined a baseball team with the help of Father Charles Keefe, who bought her a uniform. Even in those early days Lyle saw herself as an "outcast" because she rejected the traditional values and roles reserved for women. Preferring to play baseball, she resisted attending school, and her ability to find games was uncanny. Soon everybody called her Tomboy instead of Marcenia. Some, such as Gabby Street, former big-league catcher, called her a pest.

Street had led the St. Louis Cardinals to two National League pennants (1930 and 1931) and one World Series victory (1931), but when the Cards slumped in 1932 he was replaced by Frankie Frisch. Moving down to manage in the minors, Street ended up at the helm of the St. Paul Saints. There he established a baseball school, much as Kid Elberfeld had done in Atlanta. Young Marcenia Lyle hung around the school, pestering the former catcher to let her play. Resisting at first, he finally gave in and let her play—then was so impressed with Tomboy's abilities that he bought her a pair of cleats and let her attend his baseball school.

During World War II, Marcenia Lyle left St. Paul for the San Francisco Bay area to find her sister, who was a nurse in the military. This move would send her into American Legion baseball, barnstorming, the Negro League minors and, ultimately, the Negro League majors. Arriving with less than a dollar in her pocket, Lyle found herself a job, a place to live, and a baseball team, all before finding her sister.

In San Francisco Lyle gave herself the "playing name" of Toni Stone—the "Toni" because she thought it sounded like "Tomboy." From the time she stepped up to bat for Al Love's championship American Legion team, the five-foot-seven, 146-pound ballplayer was known as Toni Stone in the baseball world. "In baseball, I was accepted for who I was and what I could produce," she asserts, remembering that when she went to American Legion tryouts, Al Love asked her, "What can you do, Tone?" He then put her in center field, where, she says, "he worked me to death."

Soon Stone won a position on a semipro team, the renowned San Francisco Sea Lions, black barnstormers. In her first at-bat, she drove in two runs. But, much like Lizzie Murphy, Stone felt that the owner was holding out on her, not paying her all that he had promised, so when the team was barnstorming through New Orleans and she received a better offer, she jumped to the Black Pelicans. From there she went to the New Orleans Creoles, who offered her $300 a month.

The Creoles were already a long-established team when Maud Nelson barnstormed through Louisiana in 1922: by the time Toni Stone joined them in 1949, they were part of the Negro League minors. Playing second base for the Creoles, Stone received a fair share of publicity, hitting mainly singles. When the team was in Decatur, Alabama, to play the Black Barons in September 1949, the local paper reported that Toni Stone "has made quite a few double plays unassisted." She batted .265 in her last year with the Creoles.

ELEANOR ENGLE

When Toni Stone was signed to play for the Indianapolis Clowns, the Negro Leagues were experiencing a decline in attendance every bit as dramatic as that of the All-American Girls Baseball League, and minor league baseball found itself in the same predicament. Everywhere, fans were turning to television to watch major league games. When newspapers reported the signing of Stone in 1953, the story of Eleanor Engle was still fresh in the minds of baseball people.

On Saturday, June 21, 1952, the Class AA Harrisburg Senators of the Interstate League signed a twenty-four-year-old shortstop named Eleanor Engle. As soon as the signing was announced, there wasn't a baseball person who didn't have something to say. Howard Gordon, general manager of the Senators, assured reporters that Engle was signed "because of her ability as demonstrated in workouts at the ball park. She can hit the ball a lot better than some of the fellows on the club."

Buck Etchison, the Senators' manager, had different ideas. "I won't have a girl playing for me," he fumed. "This is a no-woman's land and believe me, I mean it. She'll play when hell freezes over." Although Engle practiced with the rest of the team, Etchison wouldn't let her sit in the dugout. In the first game the Senators played after signing Engle, the manager sent her all the way to the press box, where she sat out the game.

Up until this time, Eleanor Charlson Engle, usually referred to as Mrs. Engle by the press, had played only softball, making it doubtful that Howard Gordon was telling the whole truth about his reasons for signing her. Most likely, he wanted an attraction to boost attendance for the stuck-in-seventh-place Senators. Engle was issued a baseball uniform consisting of a short-sleeved shirt just like the other players wore—and a pair of short shorts, which the other players most definitely did not wear.

As in the case of Jackie Mitchell, the world will never know whether Eleanor Engle could have played shortstop (or any other position) in the minors. On June 23, two days after Engle signed the contract, George M. Trautman, head of the minor leagues, voided it. After first appealing to Baseball Commissioner Ford Frick for backup, Trautman declared that "such travesties" as the signing of women players "will not be tolerated." Clubs that signed or attempted to sign women would "be subject to severe penalties." On June 23, 1952, organized baseball formally banned women from the minor leagues. The directive has never been rescinded.

Engle was distraught. "Why should he do this to me?" she asked. "If I can't play baseball I don't want to do anything." She told reporters she could have played and helped the team. After the first shock, Engle announced that she would try out for the Fort Wayne Daisies of the AAGBL, managed by Jimmie Foxx. Then she faded from the scene without having played for an AAGBL team. Today she has come to public attention again in an ironic way. For their 1992 sales, Topps baseball card publishers issued an archive series. Card number 332 depicts Eleanor Engle wearing a Senators hat.

In 1953, Indianapolis Clowns owner Syd Pollack signed Stone to play second base, maintaining that he was not doing it for publicity or as a gimmick, but because she played a good brand of baseball.

The truth probably resides somewhere between the publicity and the good baseball. The reputation of the Indianapolis Clowns (originally the Ethiopian Clowns, out of Miami) was built on gimmicks of all kinds. When the Clowns finally moved to Indianapolis in 1939 and joined the Negro American League, they toned down many of their antics and stuck more to playing baseball straight. At Indianapolis's Victory Field they drew standing-room-only crowds, and at one game in Detroit's Briggs Stadium in 1948 they attracted more than 41,000 fans.

After Jackie Robinson's first year with the Brooklyn Dodgers, other major league franchises started to sign the best of young black players, effectively dooming the Negro Leagues. As early as 1951 many of the individual teams returned to barnstorming, much as Bill Allington's All-Stars were a throwback to the barnstorming Bloomer Girl teams of thirty years earlier. In 1951 young Henry Aaron played second base for the Clowns, batting .380 before his contract was purchased by the Boston Braves for $10,000. Two years later, second base was the position Syd Pollack hired Toni Stone to play. Appearing in fifty games, she batted .243.

Reaction to Stone, and her reaction to others, was mixed. "I come to play ball," she announced, bringing her old glove and shoes. "Women have got just as much right to play baseball as men," she maintains when asked about her days as a ballplayer.

Stone in publicity photo

Syd Pollack contended that he signed Stone only because she could play baseball well. Certainly the publicity she received—newspaper and magazine interviews, her picture on the Clowns' program—was the kind other ballplayers received. But Stone remembers that Pollack asked her to play in shorts; she told him she would quit baseball before she would do that.

Buster Haywood, her manager on the Clowns, believed that "it was mostly a show, that's what it was. She did pretty good, but she couldn't compete with the men to save her life. Now, in women's baseball, she would be a top player. She knew the fundamentals." Stone recalls that most of the men shunned her and gave her a hard time because she was a woman intruding in their domain. Thinking back on it today, she reflects that "They didn't mean any harm and in their way they liked me. Just that I wasn't supposed to be there. They'd tell me to go home and fix my husband some biscuits, or any damn thing. Just get the hell away from here."

Not everybody reacted by ostracizing Stone. Hall-of-Fame out-fielder Oscar Charleston, one of the great stars of the Negro Leagues, took over managing the Clowns and got along fine with her. She reserves her greatest praise for Charleston. "He was the greatest, he was fair. He'd let me get up there and hit."

The memory Stone enjoys the most is that of playing against Satchel Paige on Easter Sunday of 1953, in Omaha. "He was so good," she remembers, "that he'd ask batters where they wanted it, just so they'd have a chance. He'd ask, 'You want it high? You want it low? You want it right in the middle? Just say.' People still couldn't get a hit against him.

"I get up there and he says, 'Hey, T, how do you like it?' I said, 'It doesn't matter. Just don't hurt me.'

"When he wound up—he had these big old feet—all you could see was his shoe. I stood there shaking, but I got a hit. Right out over second base. Happiest moment in my life."

While playing in the minor leagues in 1950, Marcenia Lyle married Aurelious Alberga. A man credited with being the first black officer in the U.S. Army, Alberga had served in World War I. He didn't want his wife playing baseball. "He would have stopped me if he could," she recalls. But just as her parents couldn't stop her, just as Gabby Street couldn't get rid of her, just as her teammates couldn't drive her away if that's what they had in mind, Alberga couldn't stop Toni Stone from playing baseball.

In 1954, Pollack sold Stone's contract to the Kansas City Monarchs. Unlike the Clowns, the Monarchs had always been a serious team and at first Stone was glad to be playing for them. But soon she felt she wasn't being played enough. Although she protested, she felt there was nothing she could do about it, so at the end of the 1954 season she quit baseball and returned to Oakland, where she worked as a nurse. Her husband died in 1988, and today Marcenia Lyle Alberga still lives in the house they bought when they were married.

Living in Oakland, Alberga continued to play recreational baseball until she was sixty years old. By 1970, the generation growing up knew nothing about women who had played baseball and little about the Negro Leagues. But with the growth of official celebrations such as Black History Month and Women's History Month, African-Americans and women who want their contributions to be known have searched the far and recent past for little-known heroes.

In this context, the name of Toni Stone made headlines again during the 1980s and 1990s. In the Twin Cities she was invited to speak to young students during Black History Month, and the city of St. Paul proclaimed March 6, 1990, as "Toni Stone Day." And in 1991 the Baseball Hall of Fame honored the players of the Negro Leagues—Toni Stone included—in a ceremony, presenting each with a medallion.

Today Marcenia Lyle Alberga is no longer an outcast because she took a different road than the narrow path reserved for women. Instead she is a pioneer.

The Sun Sox

TWO EVENTS INSPIRED FORMER ATLANTA BRAVES EXECUTIVE
Bob Hope in his effort to open the doors of baseball to women.
The first came in the late 1970s, when Hope was working for the
Coca-Cola Company. Bill Veeck, owner of the Chicago White Sox,
asked that corporation to pick up the tab for a series of national
tryouts aimed at finding a woman qualified to play second base in
the majors. Hope disagreed with Veeck's approach, thinking it
was neither reasonable nor possible for an inexperienced player
to step into the bigs, but the idea of women playing baseball
stayed with him. Vacationing with his daughters in Florida a few
years later, he observed some women playing softball and was
impressed. "These women could play as well as Class A minor
league teams," he says. "I saw no reason why the best women
couldn't play at that level, and surely some women could play
better than some men. In baseball, finesse, quickness, and mobil-
ity are the issue, and women are more flexible and in better shape
than male players." Thus was born Hope's 1984 attempt to field
an entire team of female baseball players in the minor leagues—
the Sun Sox.

In the fall of 1984, the Class A Florida State League voted to expand from ten teams to twelve. When Hope learned that the Daytona Beach franchise of the FSL was open, he and his brother-in-law Major Snow went to work: they arranged for Georgia Tech baseball coach Jim Morris to conduct tryouts for their nascent team, the Sun Sox. It was Hope's belief that on a team composed of women the players would have one another for support and would thus stand a greater chance of enduring and succeeding. In September 1984, he issued a call for female ballplayers to attend tryouts.

Approximately sixty women showed up at Georgia Tech's Rose Bowl Field. At least that many reporters mobbed the scene, with the Associated Press starting its story this way: "Female athletes from around the country—united by a common dream of smashing pro baseball's sex barrier—tried out Monday for the Sun Sox, a women's team applying for admission to the Class A Florida State League."

Through his associations with major league baseball, Hope invited several scouts to the tryouts, asking them to rate the women as prospects. According to him, the scouts ranked five women as minor league prospects and one—Kim Hawkins—as a major league prospect. All the women played softball, but the six prospects had grown up playing baseball with their brothers or other boys. "I think women can play against men," Hawkins told reporters. "Men don't think so, but I do."

Reaction to Hope's initiative was mixed. Furman Bisher, a longtime sports columnist for the *Atlanta Constitution* and *The Sporting News*, opined that the Sun Sox would not qualify for the Florida State League: "First comes finding a roster of girls who can stand the gaff and play the men at their own game. A Sun Sox player will have to be able to throw the ball hard enough, hit the ball far enough, make it from first to third on the hit-and-run, or haul down a soaring drive and then crash into the outfield wall without holding up the game to fix her face."

Henry Aaron believed otherwise. As early as 1977, when he was the minor league director of the Atlanta Braves, Aaron had maintained: "There is no logical reason why [women] shouldn't play baseball. It's not that tough. Baseball is not a game of strength; hitting is not strength. The game needs a special kind of talent, thinking and timing. Some women, as well as some men, qualify in that respect. . . . A ball going 90 miles an hour can be knocked over the fence by anyone sticking a bat out and making perfect contact." Hope asked Aaron to be the player personnel director of the Sun Sox and Aaron accepted.

Neither Bob Hope nor Major Snow backed down from the import of what they were doing. "Our intent is to make this a minor league opportunity for women to play professional baseball," Hope informed the media. "The major problem is not whether women can play Class A baseball, but that they've never been given a chance." Snow said that once the Sun Sox were a franchised team, more women would hear about them and come to future tryouts, giving the Sox a larger recruiting base. "Our goal," he said, "is to have several of our players graduate to teams in higher classifications and eventually be responsible for the first woman in the big leagues."

Coach Jim Morris worked out the women and made the first cut, narrowing the field to twenty-five. Kim Hawkins, then a twenty-

year-old truck driver, remembers that "Morris was great. He treated us well." None of the women had ever played with wooden
bats. "If you didn't hit the ball right, it stung your hands," Hawkins
says, "but if you hit it right, it felt really good." She also recalls
that some of the women, used to a much smaller softball diamond,
couldn't make the infield throws.

When Aaron appeared at Georgia Tech's field to observe the
tryouts, he walked into the dugout and the women cheered. "I
said all along, ten years ago, that it can be done," he told them.
"Good luck to you." Speaking to reporters, he evaluated the players and their situation by saying, "This is amazing. A few of them
can handle themselves. They're going to have to give them a
chance to play."

"They" meant the board of directors of the Florida State
League, which would vote on whether or not to grant the Daytona
Beach franchise to the Sun Sox. Questioned by reporters, FSL
spokesmen said they were keeping an open mind and weren't dis-
counting the Sox.

Back at Georgia Tech, Jim Morris continued to put the hopefuls
through the paces—hitting, running, fielding, sliding. His goal
was to come up with nineteen women good enough to play Class A
ball. That number proved unrealistic, however, and Hope and
Snow sought to fill out their roster with male players. "We firmly
believe our responsibility is to give women a legitimate starting
point in pro baseball," said Snow, "and [we] will take into consid-
eration the lack of training women have had by not being allowed
into amateur baseball past the Little League level."

The two men were quite optimistic about their chances of being accepted by the Florida State League. "They're definitely treating us seriously," Hope told reporters, adding that he was "90 percent certain" the Sun Sox would win approval when voting took place the next week.

But a few signs to the contrary began leaking out. Spokesmen for the FSL suggested to the press that perhaps the Sun Sox would play sixty games a year (a half-schedule), all of them exhibition games—in short, not one official game. When pressed for a reason why this "exhibition half-schedule" would apply to the Sun Sox, one FSL spokesman replied, "I think after somebody sees them get beat 25–0 or 30–0, that will be the end of that." When the board of directors met, they voted to award the Daytona Beach franchise to a team from Tennessee, even though, according to Hope, that team had not applied within the deadline period.

Bob Hope, founder of Sun Sox

Bob Hope was stunned, as was Major Snow.

After recovering from the shock, the two men tried to purchase some other minor league franchise as a home for the Sox. The offers poured in from Florida, California, North Carolina, and elsewhere, but the asking price was three or four times what it would have been had the Sun Sox been a regular Class A team of men. "The issue, to me," Hope told the press, "is much bigger than just buying a baseball team. Is there a spot where women and men can play coed sports, together, on a professional level? I think it's a meaningful human rights issue. I'd definitely like to see it done for next season." But next season came and still the Sox couldn't find a franchise; in March 1985, Hope and his backers finally gave up.

Bob Hope believes that many twelve-year-old girls are the stars of their Little League teams because they are physically and mentally committed to baseball and have hung in there despite all odds. "Then, there is no place to go," he says. "It becomes unfashionable to play. But women will do it if there is a reason to play, such as the existence of a minor league team." When the Sun Sox were denied a franchise, the female players once again had no place to go. They returned to their jobs and to softball.

When asked what prevents women from playing in the minors, Hope replies that "the level of prejudice is what stands in the way." Hope kept the Sun Sox uniforms and dozens of hats, thinking that maybe some day, somewhere, baseball will be open to women. Meanwhile, he ponders an unpleasant lesson. "People can be cooperative," he says, "and still keep you out."

AGAIN THE MINOR LEAGUES

In August 1971, with the minor league season almost over, twenty-three-year-old Gloria Jean "Jackie" Jackson, five-foot-seven and 140 pounds, tried out for the Pittsfield Senators. No stranger to sports, Jackson had been voted the outstanding female athlete in her senior class at Andover High, in Linthicum, Maryland. By 1971 the outstanding male athlete of the senior class, Jim Spencer, was the first baseman for the California Angels. Jackie Jackson was a first baseman, too—in a men's softball league, where she says she learned to take verbal harassment.

Jackson had always wanted to be a major league player, but "just didn't know how to go about it before." Thinking that the last-place Senators should and maybe would be interested in new ideas and new players, she called Pat McKernan, the junior-high teacher who owned the team, and suggested he give her a tryout. At first speechless, McKernan then thought, "Why not? There's no law that I know of to prevent women from trying out."

Because newspaper, radio, and television reporters of all kinds were present at the event, Jackson was "scared stiff." During her short tryout, she played the outfield and first base, performing well in the field, less well with the bat, and poorly at running the bases (five seconds from home to first).

Asked about her performance, Jackson answered: "I couldn't put enough wood on the ball, although I did sting a few. I don't want to alibi, but I think I would have done better if I had used a lighter bat." Referring to the media coverage, owner McKernan argued that "Mickey Mantle would have had a tough time to impress anyone under the circumstances."

"I was good," Jackson said in an interview fifteen years later. "They told me I had the best hands of everybody they'd seen. The owner wanted me to travel with the team—without a contract. He said I should have had a contract, but I was a woman. I said we could sue baseball. He said, 'I'm a married man, I have two children, I'm a junior-high-school teacher. I don't need the aggravation.'" She and McKernan parted on good terms.

The next day, Jackson received a call from the owner of the minor league Raleigh-Durham Triangles. He asked her to play for the Triangles and appear in their starting lineup and she accepted. One day later the owner called her again, to revoke the offer. "A week after that," says Jackie, "he lost his franchise."

Today Jackson, who owns and operates her own market research firm, believes that her tryout did have an impact on society, particularly on the Little League battles that came to a head three years later. "There will be women in major league baseball," she predicts. "Women can compete at that level. You don't have to be six-foot-six to be a force in baseball." All it will take, she argues, is girls who are given the chance to "eat, sleep, and live baseball."

Gera and Postema

IN UMPIRE SCHOOL BERNICE GERA PROMPTLY BEGAN TO chat with players who spoke to her. "Bernice!" bellowed the instructor, "you can't do that!" As punishment, he assigned her two pushups for the first offense. Alone in her Florida hotel room at night, the sole female student was subjected to a different kind of treatment: drunken men threw beer bottles at her door and cursed the woman who wanted to be an umpire. After scoring high on the written test, Gera had a difficult time away from the rule book. Greeted with pleasantry, she strayed from the task at hand; greeted with hostility, she felt she couldn't do her job. After fighting organized baseball for five years and winning a legal victory for women, Bernice Gera walked off the job.

Married to Steven Gera, a photographer for the New York highway department, Bernice spent much of her time helping children learn baseball skills. She would save enough money to buy twenty or thirty baseball tickets, then round up that many kids and take them to a major league game. At Rockaway Park, in New York City, she paid to throw baseballs at carnival-stand attractions, over the years winning 350 stuffed animals that she gave to children. A self-acclaimed hitter of the long ball, she staged hitting

contests with Roger Maris and others, the proceeds going to charity. Throughout the 1960s, Gera tried to get a job in baseball. "I
love baseball so much I'd do anything, even shine [the players']
shoes," she declared. But the guardians of the game consistently
turned her down. Finally, one day in 1967 she decided to become
a baseball umpire.

Graduation from an accredited umpire's school is a prereq-
uisite for umpiring in the minor and major leagues. Wanting a job
in organized baseball, Gera applied to the well-known Al Somers
Umpire School. In light of what occurred later, it seems amazing
that she was accepted—until it's understood that Somers misread
her name as "Bernie." When she called him on the phone he recognized his mistake and promptly returned her check, saying that
no woman ever had or ever would attend his school.

Rejected by Somers, Gera applied to Jim Finley's Florida Baseball Umpire School. Upon receiving her application, Finley suggested she take a course of home study, but Gera persisted and
he finally allowed her to attend. After graduating and returning
to Jackson Heights, in Queens, she officiated high school, charity, and semipro games for two years, gaining experience. Early
in 1969 she wrote to every minor league along the East Coast,
requesting an umpire's application form. Only the Florida State
League replied with a form.

Wanting to work closer to home, Bernice wrote directly to Vincent McNamara, president of the Class A New York–Pennsylvania
League, who replied that he couldn't hire her because dressing
room facilities in ballparks were inadequate for women and
because the players used foul language that women should not

Bernice Gera

hear. "I've umpired a lot of games and I don't think I could hear anything new," Gera retorted. "As for dressing room facilities, I notice that the racetracks have been able to take care of the lady jockeys."

At this point Bernice Gera was offered legal help by Representative Mario Biaggi of the Bronx. After being contacted by Biaggi and Gera several times, McNamara sent Gera a contract to umpire in the New York–Penn League starting in July 1969. Letters of congratulations poured in to the would-be umpire, and the press ran a photo of her smiling and holding her contract with a thumbs-up signal.

One day before she was to umpire her first minor league game, Bernice Gera received a lengthy telegram from Philip Piton, president of the National Association of Professional Baseball Leagues (the minor league system), informing her in legal terms that her contract was being rescinded. Like Commissioner Kenesaw Mountain Landis, Piton "voided" the legal contract offered a woman. Unlike Landis, he declined to comment on his reasons for doing so.

But Piton and those he represented underestimated Bernice Gera. When it came to fighting on the legal level, she held on with bulldog determination, exposing the untenable arguments of the baseball hierarchy. With the help of Mario Biaggi, she took the issue to the New York State Human Rights Commission, arguing that her civil rights had been violated.

In October 1969, with the baseball season over, minor league representatives appeared before the commission. Barney Deary, administrator of the umpire development program, said that women would be approved if they met the league's height, weight, and age requirements—a minimum height of five feet, ten inches, a minimum weight of 175 pounds, and an age range of 24–35. Bernice Gera was 38 years old, stood five-foot-two, and weighed 129 pounds. According to government Health, Education and Welfare statistics, only 0.6 percent of American women met the minor league's qualifications. In addition, argued Biaggi, former umpire Vincent McNamara as well as Hall-of-Fame umpire Bill Klem had not met the height-weight-age specifications "without any indication of deficiency in the quality of their performance."

Ruling that Gera's civil rights had been violated, the Human Rights Commission ordered the minor leagues to "cease and desist from refusing to employ any individual because of her sex and to establish new physical standards which have a reasonable relation to the requirements of the duties of an umpire." The NAPBL appealed the Human Rights Commission's decision to the State Supreme Court Appellate Division, which by a 3–2 vote upheld the HRC ruling, and again organized baseball appealed the ruling. After the HRC ruled for a third time that Gera's rights were being violated and the NAPBL looked no closer to hiring her than before, she and her attorney filed a $25 million lawsuit against the baseball commissioner, the NAPBL, and the New York–Penn League on March 15, 1971.

Approximately one year later, without stating its reasons for doing so, organized baseball rendered Gera an umpire's contract. Like the 1969 contract, this one, too, was with the New York–Penn League, and Gera was told to report to work on June 23, 1972. Although jubilant over her legal victory, she confessed to the press that she was a bit worried about her fellow umpires. "Umpiring is a team job," she told the press. "They can hang you if they want to."

In Class A, games are officiated by two umpires. Bernice Gera and Douglas Hartmeyer, both rookies, were scheduled to officiate the season opener between Geneva and Auburn in Geneva, New York. That game was postponed by rain, and a June 24 doubleheader became the season opener. Gera came to the umpire's meeting and then took the field as the bases umpire, her partner going behind plate. A sellout crowd of over three thousand came to witness the event and at least one newspaper reported that Gera received a large ovation during the pregame announcements.

The first few innings went smoothly. Then came the fourth. With a runner on second, the Auburn batter hit a line drive to the Geneva second baseman, who promptly threw to the shortstop covering second, trying to turn a double play before the runner could return to the bag. "Safe!" called Gera—and then, a second later, "Out!"

The second call brought Auburn manager Nolan Campbell charging from the dugout to confront the blue-suited official. "Why did you change your call?" he shouted at her.

"I made a mistake," she answered, explaining that she forgot it was a force play.

"That was the second mistake," snapped Campbell. "The first was putting on that uniform." When Campbell then suggested that Gera go back to the kitchen and peel potatoes, she gave him the thumb. "You're not only a woman," he quipped upon ejection, "but you've got a quick temper." Speaking to reporters later, Campbell said, "I never said any cuss words to her. It surprised me when she threw me out."

The first game continued, with Gera looking strained. When it was over, she walked into the office of Geneva general manager Joe McDonough and announced, "I've just resigned from baseball. I'm sorry, Joe." In tears, Bernice Gera walked out to her car and departed.

One of the great prejudices against women is the sexist adage

"Within the space of a week man got to the moon and woman became an umpire. Well, that's life, boys. You win one and you lose one.

"I don't know which event is more significant, but I notice that the moon is still going strong. I doubt if we'll be able to say the same for baseball now that milady has got her tooties in the door.

"And that she has. Mrs. Bernice Gera, a 37-year-old Long Island housewife, has been hired by the Class A New York–Pennsylvania League. Rather than risk Mrs. Gera's lawsuit charging it with discrimination, the league agreed to let her umpire. Personally, I think the league should have risked World War III.

"Nothing personal, pet, but this step is guaranteed to change the entire shape of baseball for all time. After lady umpires, of course, will come lady players, lady managers, lady scouts, lady bullpen coaches. And in no time at all, baseball will go the way of canasta. . . .

"While I can suffer lady golfers, lady shot putters, lady jockeys and lady rasslers, I'm opposed to lady umpires tooth and nailfile.

"Women are congenitally unable to umpire a baseball game because:

"1. Women are congenitally unable to resist a compliment. . . .

"2. Women are congenitally unable to leave well enough alone. . . ."

—Tim Horgan, *Sunday Herald Traveler*,
July 27, 1969

that "a woman always changes her mind." Many umpires believe that in order to maintain authority over the game, they must never change a call. Thus for Gera to change her call during her very first game was a crime for which there was no forgiveness in baseball. Her rookie partner pontificated to reporters afterward: "Saying you've made a mistake is very unethical in our profession. That's one thing you never do. You never reverse yourself."

But Gera had done something far worse than change her call. She had just left the players and fans in the lurch. Umpires owe commitment to the game, not to their own comfort or feelings. It is their responsibility to assure that the game is played fairly and called correctly. By leaving the teams with no second umpire for the second half of the doubleheader, Bernice Gera walked out on her primary responsibility for the evening. Fortunately for the players and fans, when the call went out for another umpire, there was one sitting in the stands.

While she didn't admit it at the time, years later Gera acknowledged that she knew before stepping onto the field that she would quit that night. The reason she gave was that during the umpires' meeting nobody would talk to her and that Hartmeyer wouldn't discuss signals with her. Blaming the "cool resentment" of her fellow umpires and the entire baseball establishment, Gera announced: "I quit after the game because I was physically, mentally, and financially drained. . . . it is hard to get used to having people spit at you and threaten your life."

After resigning as umpire, Gera continued to put on baseball exhibits. In 1975 she was hired by the New York Mets to work in group tickets sales and handle the Lady Mets Club, a social organization devoted to lunching, meeting ballplayers, and watching baseball games.

After four years Gera resigned from the Mets. Soon after, she and her husband moved to Florida. Bernice had plans to work with a promoter who was going to develop the Bernice Gera Sports Complex, where she could teach baseball to boys and girls. That deal fell through, but the couple stayed in Florida. There, after a long battle with cancer, Bernice Gera died in 1992. "In a way, they succeeded in getting rid of me," she used to say. "But in a way, I've succeeded too. I've broken the barrier. It can be done."

Pam Postema at umpire-training school

IN 1976, WHEN BERNICE GERA WAS HISTORY AND A young woman named Christine Wren was umpiring games in the Class A Northwest League, twenty-two-year-old Pam Postema applied to the Al Somers Umpire School in Florida. Somers didn't answer Postema's letter. So she wrote him a second time and this time he replied, stating that his school didn't have the proper "facilities" for women. When the would-be umpire found his house and knocked on his front door, Somers promised her he would "think about it." Later he and former National League umpire Harry Wendelstedt, chief instructor at the school, interviewed Postema and accepted her into the school.

The daughter of a farmer who says his daughter has the right personality for umpiring—independent, stubborn, and determined—Pam Postema grew up in Willard, Ohio, playing catch with her brother and playing third base on a local baseball team. After graduation from high school she worked at a string of low-paying jobs until her mother told her about umpire Christine Wren and suggested that Pam might be interested in doing the same thing.

That was when Postema applied to the Al Somers Umpire School. For the 1977 winter session, 130 students were admitted to the six-week course. Of these, thirty either quit or were sent packing. One of those who stayed and learned was Postema, who graduated high in her class. Then she spent three months looking for local high school, college, and semipro games to umpire. Just when she had given up hope of umpiring for pay, she received a call from George MacDonald, president of the Gulf Coast League and the Florida State League, offering her a job in the rookie-class Gulf Coast League. A former umpire himself with eighteen years in the minors, MacDonald had been the only person to send Bernice Gera an application form back in 1969.

Working games in the rookie league, Postema began to learn professional umpiring in trial-by-fire. She experienced her first in-your-face confrontation when manager Joe Jones of the White Sox rushed out of the dugout, thrust his nose an inch away from hers, and began to shout. "I was shocked," she says. "I couldn't believe anybody could yell that loud and be, well, that rude. I had never seen anyone that mad before."

When the rookie season ended, MacDonald offered Postema a chance to umpire during the last few weeks of the Florida State League. She did well, learning along the way, and in 1978 she returned to umpire in the Gulf Coast League for a second season.

In 1979 MacDonald then moved her up to the Class A Florida State League, and he repeated the assignment the following year.

After two years in the rookie league and two in Class A, the twenty-six-year-old umpire, now the only woman umpire in baseball (Christine Wren's contract had not been renewed), was assigned to the Class AA Texas League, an important step upward. At the end of her sixth year in baseball, Postema was moved to the Triple-A Pacific Coast League.

In the minor leagues the most significant upward move is the one to Triple-A, and Postema was ecstatic that she had made it. Understanding the magnitude of the move, the media covered the situation in full. Al Somers, who had once vowed he would never allow a woman in his school, even sent her a note of congratulations.

In Triple-A ball, a crew of three umpires works each game. Here the job of calling balls and strikes is somewhat easier than in the lower minors because the pitching is so much better. Still, players and managers challenge the umpire and, if they heap personal abuse on the officials in blue or try to wrest control of the game from them, face ejection. During her years in baseball, Postema ejected more managers and players than was average for whatever league she was in: she once ejected a batboy and she came close to ejecting a mascot, the Philly Phanatic. She believes that as a woman she was subject to more abuse from the players and managers and therefore had to act to establish her control of the game.

Larry Gerlach, author of *The Men in Blue* and chair of the Society for American Baseball Research's Umpires and Rules

Triple-A umpire Postema

Pam Postema

Committee, observed Postema's umpiring in the Pacific Coast League. "She excelled in working the plate and running the game, the principal make-or-break criteria for a major league umpire," he says. "Later, Postema passed two critical tests when she worked the Hall of Fame game: players, press, and fans praised her performance and, most important, few spectators or reporters knew it was a woman behind the plate." Gerlach, a professor of sports history, concludes that "Postema succeeded in becoming invisible on the field, but remained a female to the Lords of Baseball."

Becoming invisible on the field wasn't easy, and Postema believes she never completely achieved it. Throughout her career she felt that most managers, players, and fellow umpires could never see her as an umpire, only as a female. Thus they treated her in ways they would never treat male umpires, and their abuse frequently consisted of put-downs of women. One manager at a Triple-A level grabbed the umpire at the plate, swept off her mask, tilted her backward, and kissed her, trying to insert his tongue into her mouth. She was so taken aback that she failed to eject him, and regrets that she didn't. On another occasion, players and managers left a frying pan at home plate for her, with a note telling her she knew where she could go with it.

Not all of Postema's experiences were confrontations, and many were rewarding. When she worked major league spring training games, pitchers such as Ed Farmer and catchers such as Ozzie Virgil praised her work behind the plate, and manager Chuck Tanner said he saw no reason why she shouldn't be in the bigs. Barney Deary and others who decide to move umpires up or release them from their contracts generally reported to the press that Postema did well behind the plate. In 1987, Deary informed the *New York Times*, "I haven't had one problem with her, and I understand she's still rated as a prospect."

A prospect is one who might make the major leagues. As she moved up through the ranks of organized ball, it was always Postema's goal to make the majors. But she was kept at the Triple-A level for six years, an inordinately long time. In 1988 she was invited to umpire major league spring-training games, and all seemed to be going smoothly. Even though Astros pitcher Bob Knepper spoke out against women in baseball, his stance hurt him more than it hurt the umpire. Later that year National League president Bart Giamatti invited Postema to umpire the annual Hall of Fame game at Cooperstown, that year between the Yankees and the Braves. In both spring training and the Hall of Fame game Postema was impressive, but for whatever reasons, Giamatti did not promote her, although she was once again invited to umpire spring training in 1989. In the summer of that year, Giamatti died from a heart attack. With his death, the thirty-five-year-old umpire with thirteen years in the minors felt that her chance of making the majors had perished. She was right: in December the Triple-A Alliance released her from baseball. The woman who would not quit was fired.

At first too stunned to act, Postema eventually filed a federal sex discrimination lawsuit, suing the National and American leagues, the Triple-A Alliance, and the Baseball Office for Umpire Development. "I believe that I belong in the major leagues," she said. "If it weren't for the fact that I'm a woman, I would be there right now." Her demands include back pay and installation as an umpire in the major leagues.

In 1992 she published a book, *You've Got to Have Balls to Make It in This League.* In it, she praised many fellow umpires who helped her, including Doug Harvey (who at the time of Gera believed women couldn't umpire), Joe West, Mark Hirschbeck, Eric Gregg, Steve Palermo, Tim Tschida, and Rocky Roe. She also praised a few players such as Bobby Bonds, Bobby Bonilla, Jose Canseco, and Brett Butler. But they were exceptions, and Postema concluded that "Almost all of the people in the baseball community don't want anyone interrupting their little male-dominated way of life. . . . And I'll never understand why it's easier for a female to become an astronaut or cop or fire fighter or soldier or Supreme Court justice than it is to become a major league umpire."

On March 14, 1989, Pam Postema umpired behind the plate during a spring training game between the Houston Astros and the Pittsburgh Pirates in Kissimmee, Florida. Astros pitcher Bob Knepper hurled five scoreless innings against the Pirates. After the game, Knepper stood outside the Astros clubhouse (he would not conduct press interviews inside the locker room when a female sports reporter was present) and made the following statement:

"I just don't think a woman should be an umpire. There are certain things a woman shouldn't be and an umpire is one of them. It's a physical thing. God created women to be feminine. I don't think they should be competing with men.

"It has nothing to do with her ability. I don't think women should be in any position of leadership. I don't think they should be presidents or politicians. I think women were created not in an inferior position, but in a role of submission to men. You can be a woman umpire if you want, but that doesn't mean it's right. You can be a homosexual if you want, but that doesn't mean that's right either.

"It's her choice what she wants to do with her life, and I'm not going to give her a hard time. I'll respect her more because she's a woman. I'm not going to condemn her. But if God is unhappy with her, she's going to have to deal with that later."

Julie Croteau

NEARLY ONE HUNDRED YEARS FROM THE TIME THE FIRST
bloomer teams strode onto the ball fields and into public notice, a
young woman named Julie Croteau made headlines by playing
college ball on an otherwise-male team. As an eighteen-year-old
freshman in the spring of 1989, Croteau played first base for the
Seahawks of St. Mary's College in Maryland, and her debut was
covered by eleven news organizations. Three years later the first
baseman made headlines again, this time because she quit the
team and took a leave of absence from college. For this ballplayer, the treatment of women in baseball was part of a larger
question—the gender division of sports during the formative
years.

Born December 4, 1970, Julie Croteau grew up in Prince
William County, Virginia, and began playing T-ball at the age
of six, two years after girls had won the right to play in Little
League. At age eight she entered Little League, where she batted
.300 and her coach said of her, "as a first baseman, from a defensive point of view she was one of our best." Although neither Ray
nor Nancy Croteau were baseball fans, they were pleased that
their daughter loved the sport so much. From Little League Julie

progressed to Major League (ages 13–15) and also played in a fall baseball league for fourteen-year-olds. She began to attend baseball clinics at thirteen and at sixteen entered the Babe Ruth League (ages 16–18), playing there until she was seventeen and a senior in high school. During those years, says her father, she "had teeth cracked and her nose busted, all kinds of bumps, bruises, twisted ankles, just like anybody else. She's a good ballplayer, just like the guys."

At Osbourn Park high school, the five-foot-seven, 122-pound lefty tried out for the junior varsity baseball team. The JV coach phoned Julie's parents and suggested that their daughter take up softball. Nancy and Ray Croteau were angered. "The coaches didn't call the boys and suggest that they change sports," says Nancy Croteau. "They didn't tell them to go play golf." When it became clear that Julie wasn't going to take up softball, the coach accepted her on the JV team. She had hoped to play first base, at least part of the time, but the coach moved an outfielder to that bag and benched Croteau. "I felt like the coach was embarrassed to have me on his team," she says. "It was as if having a girl on the team was bad enough, but having a girl who could start would be a putdown on the school."

During her junior year Croteau tried out for the JV team again, but wasn't accepted. As a senior she tried out for the varsity baseball team, the Osbourn Park Yellow Jackets. After the coach cut Julie from the team, Nancy and Ray Croteau, both lawyers, filed a lawsuit asking that she be reinstated.

That was when Julie Croteau first made national headlines, and soon reporters were interviewing everybody connected with her career. "She's a young lady with a lot of heart and fortitude and the skills to go along with it," said the coach of her Big League team. "I think she's just as capable of playing first base as many of the boys." Ross Natolli, the baseball coach at Catholic University, where Julie had taken a series of clinics, believed that "She has average high school ability for boys. She's a line drive hitter, and she makes good contact. I'm seeing seventy to eighty high school games a year, and she has enough ability to make most high school teams."

Twelve of the seventeen members of the Yellow Jackets appeared in federal court to support their coach, while the remaining five delivered a letter to the press, proclaiming, "We don't in any way back the plaintiff. Not because she is female, but because we feel this suit has no grounds at all. . . . Our job is to win baseball games utilizing the best seventeen athletes. We feel we have the best seventeen, bar none." In publishing the letter, most newspapers duly recorded the 4–13–1 record of the Yellow Jackets, casting some doubt on the young men's claim to have "the best seventeen, bar none."

Ultimately the U.S. district court judge handling the case ruled against Croteau. In his opinion Title IX, the federal statute that prohibits sex discrimination in school programs receiving federal funds, did not apply to the case. Mike Zitz, a reporter covering the trial, remembers how terrible he felt watching the proceedings, and how when the judge announced that there was no constitutional right to get to first base, "the entire Osbourn team jumped up and down like they were in the World Series."

In addition to being a reporter, Zitz was manager of the

Julie Croteau of the semipro Fredericksburg Giants

Fredericksburg Giants of the Virginia Baseball League. He recalls that when the verdict was read, Julie Croteau "was crushed. I could see how much she loved baseball and I couldn't live with myself if I didn't give her a chance to . . . see what she could do." So he invited Croteau to try out for the Giants.

Elated with the opportunity to be evaluated as just a ballplayer, Croteau tried out for and made the Fredericksburg Giants in the summer of 1988 and has continued to play with the semipro team every season but one since then. The team ranks consist of those who have played minor league ball and those who are going to play minor league ball, as well as college and sometimes high school students.

Around the same time that Julie lost her court case and earned a spot on the Giants, St. Mary's College of Maryland accepted her as a student with the understanding that if she could make the school's NCAA Division III baseball team, the administration and coach would do nothing to stop her. That fall, Croteau practiced with the Seahawks and in the spring she made the team.

The Seahawks knew that their opening game, in March 1989, would be covered by national news cameras because a woman was playing in an NCAA game. Players were tense, Julie Croteau included. The game was rained out, delaying the dreaded event and making everybody tenser still. Finally the team played its season opener against Spring Garden College of Philadelphia, losing 4–1. The Seahawks' leading pitcher of the previous season was so nervous that his first fifteen pitches were balls. Croteau went 0 for 3 but didn't strike out, and she fielded six chances flawlessly. "I kept thinking about the fifteen cameras," she said.

Jack Bilbee, coach of the opposing team, told reporters: "I thought she was one of their better players. Especially with two strikes on her. She really hung in there." Charley Bolen, Seahawks third baseman and team captain, admitted, "There was a lot of pressure, but we all pulled together. If a girl is as good as Julie, she deserves to be on the team. I think everyone feels she's a good addition to our team. She has good character, and she's a good person."

At first Croteau felt that fans came to judge her as a player with the intention of judging all women by her performance alone. After several weeks, she felt less pressure to represent all womankind. Even from the time she was in high school, however, she always recognized that her actions would affect other girls and women who wanted to play baseball. Her playing college baseball "sends a message to high schools," she told reporters. "If it's all right at college, it should be all right at high schools and middle schools." As the Seahawks' second-string first baseman, Croteau batted .222. Under long-time coach Hal Willard, the team struggled to a 1–20–1 record.

Looking back on her first season, Julie Croteau reflects that "what happened is that for some reason I was this hero and everyone accepted it and the media covered it and the media and school were telling everyone it was a great thing, let's not destroy it. So everyone believed it." At the end of the first year, the coverage stopped: this particular baseball player was no longer news. "When the media went away, so did the message."

Instead of receiving feedback on how good it was to have a woman playing baseball, the school and team received no feedback and things went back to normal. And Julie began to think about what she saw all around her: that sports in general are considered a male privilege and birthright, and that women who want to participate in mainstream sports—"We'd have to call them men's sports," says Croteau—are dissuaded, derailed, and thwarted every step of the way. Thinking about the big questions of women and sports and society disturbed her: she felt she needed time to get away and think. She thought of quitting the team and school her junior year, but didn't do so because she felt it would be unfair to her teammates. When the 1991 season ended, she quit.

Newspapers carrying the story reported that Croteau quit baseball because her teammates read aloud articles from *Penthouse* magazine and used obscene slang referring to female genitalia as standard baseball lingo. "What I said and what the media covered were two different things," maintains Croteau. "I was talking about a problem with all sports, and I used my experiences as an example. But they wrote it as if I was criticizing my team and my school and baseball, not the general situation of all sports." Croteau says she has heard far worse than *Penthouse* articles outside of baseball, and no words she heard on the field would make her quit.

For the next fourteen months, Julie took her leave of absence, working three months as an intern for the Women's Sports Foundation and appearing as an extra in the film *A League of Their Own*. She considers meeting the AAGBL players and learning about their league one of the highlights of working on the film.

In the summer of 1992, Croteau was playing baseball with the

Fredericksburg Giants once again, and that fall she began her senior year at St. Mary's College. No longer on the Seahawks, she is still passionate about baseball, as she is about social justice. At one time she wanted to be a civil rights attorney, but today she's wondering whether there might be a better way for her to help break down the gender barriers in sports, possibly by working in sports administration. As a high school senior, Julie Croteau believed there would some day be a woman in the major leagues. Asked whether she still thinks so, she responds immediately. "I do believe it. I really do."

Starting out as a ballplayer, Croteau became interested in more than professional baseball. It's the nationwide school system she's most concerned with. "Most people don't go on to play professional sports," she points out. "They play high school sports, and there shouldn't be gender divisions in high school sports. Let students play according to their abilities, not their sex." It's true that today girls can play in Little League, but what about afterward? "They usually cut you off [in high school]. And when they cut you off in high school, they cut you off for college."

At one time major league teams signed players directly from high school and sent them into the minors. A few exceptions, such as Bob Feller and Robin Yount, came directly from high school into the bigs. Since the 1960s, however, college ball has become a training ground nearly equivalent to the minors. Today most top high school prospects go to college and play baseball. Some of them, such as Jim Abbott, play major league ball immediately after graduation. Most college players, such as Frank Thomas of the White Sox, spend a year or so in the high minors.

Today women who want to play baseball will seek to do so in high school and college, where, unlike in the minor leagues, there is no formal directive against them. Julie Croteau knows of three high school women who have applied to play baseball in college next year and haven't been turned down. She hopes her experience will help these women. "I'll do everything I can to keep them there," she promises.

LITTLE LEAGUE

Founded in Williamsport, Pennsylvania, in 1939, the Little League grew rapidly in the years after World War II. Born the same year the organization was founded, Carl Yastrzemski became the first Little Leaguer elected to the Hall of Fame for his major league feats. Today more than 75 percent of all major leaguers have played Little League ball, which for its first thirty-five years excluded girls.

Even during the conservative 1950s, some girls tried to play in Little League. Mort Leve, a former college baseball player who spent one year in the White Sox farm system, became a coach in all phases of amateur baseball, from Little League through Pony League, Colt League, and American Legion. Coaching Little League in 1951, Leve was all set to accept a girl who had tried out for the team. "She had the ability," he says, "but was ruled out" by existing regulations. During the 1950s, girls sat and cheered while their brothers got to play.

With the changed social consciousness of the 1960s, parents and daughters found themselves reasoning, arguing, demanding, and petitioning that local Little League chapters allow girls to play baseball. Because the national organization resisted admitting girls, many bitter battles were waged in thousands of communities across the nation. A typical case was that of Sharon Poole of Haverhill, Massachusetts. In July 1971, Donald Sciu-to, president of the local Little League, recruited twelve-year-old Sharon to play for the Indians on the recommendation of her nine-year-old brother, Michael. Batting cleanup in her first game, Sharon walked once, singled to drive in a run, and struck out once; she also scored once. Playing center field, she caught everything that came to her.

After the Indians defeated the Twins, 7–5, the Twins' manager protested that, according to regulations, girls were not permitted to play. Nearly fifty years after Margaret Gisolo helped lead the Blanford Cubs to victory over the Clinton Baptists, things hadn't changed much. The next night the Haverhill Indians, with Sharon on the team, defeated the Yankees, 2–1.

Julie Croteau and St. Mary's Seahawks teammates

That was the last straw: Haverhill team managers met and voted to kick Sharon off the Indians and out of the Little League. Not stopping there, they fired Donald Sciuto as Indian manager and as president of the local Little League.

Around the country girls wanted to play the real thing, but Little League officials remained entrenched, contending at each round of the struggle that girls should not play baseball because, if they did, they would be injured in their "vital parts." By March 1974, parents had filed sex-discrimination suits against the Little League in fifteen states. In Wilmington, Delaware, former Phillies pitcher and manager Dallas Green, then manager of the New York Yankees, filed on behalf of his nine-year-old daughter, Kimberly. The social tide had not merely turned, it had become a bore tide rushing upriver to inundate the Williamsport headquarters. Finally, after parents threatened to go to court to remove the Little League's congressional charter, the league abandoned its boys-only policy on June 12, 1974, "in deference to a change in social climate."

Today thousand of girls play Little League baseball each year—and many play it superlatively. Nine-year old Brianne "Breezy" Stepherson of Malden, Massachusetts, pitched nine games for the Mohawks in 1989 and in thirty-six innings, she didn't allow a single run to score, gave up just two hits, and struck out an astounding ninety-eight batters. As for hit-ting, she batted .685 and hit twelve home runs. Her vital body parts, so often mentioned by the Little League officials, remained uninjured.

The court rulings that forced Little League to admit girls opened up the game of baseball at its crucial elementary level. Unless you grow up playing hardball, it's extremely unlikely you will develop the skills to play it later. From Maud Nelson to Jean Faut to Julie Croteau, female baseball players played the real thing from their earliest days. With the Little League victory, the sex-barrier ramparts were cracked.

Epilogue

IF BASEBALL HAD BEEN OPEN TO WOMEN FOR THE LAST 150 years, we would have already seen female major leaguers. The game is closed to women not because women can't play, but because the men in power don't want women around.

The 1952 minor league directive prohibiting the signing of women exists because without such a threat against each minor league team, women would have been signed to play in organized baseball. Courageous men who believe in justice and fight for equality are present in the game—Henry Aaron is a hero for more than his baseball record; George MacDonald hired Pam Postema and an African-American umpire when nobody else would; Bob Hope risked ridicule in formulating a plan to integrate the minor leagues. If the policy of not hiring women in the minors didn't exist, some enterprising team owner, some farsighted and fair manager, some impartial scout would sign a woman, two women, three. Some of these women would have considerable skills, would improve them, and would stick out the sexism because they loved baseball.

The national pastime is a team sport. To the frustration of all

fantasy players this means that adding up team statistics doesn't automatically produce the name of the division, pennant, and World Series winner. No team has the best player in all of major league baseball at each of the nine positions. And if such a team did exist, it wouldn't necessarily win the pennant. If the 1991 World Series between the formerly last-place Atlanta Braves and the formerly last-place Minnesota Twins proved anything, it proved the importance of team chemistry.

The variables of a team sport leap over simple logic and defy mathematical columns. Team play fuses individual elements into something new that transcends the sum of its parts, that brings fans to their feet and inspires sportswriters to new paeans of victory and glory. On winning teams there are the well and the wounded, the too-old and too-green, the behemoths and the pint-sized, the solid and the shaky. In baseball, there is room for the other half of the human race—the hidden past of women at play proves it.

Baseball's last barrier will be broken. Women by the millions will view the film *A League of Their Own* and be inspired, as will men. Each year thousands of girls play Little League baseball, and surely some of them will develop into capable ballplayers wanting both the thrills and paychecks of big-leaguers. Bill Tanton of the *Baltimore Evening Sun* put it this way: "We will see a woman in the majors . . . and when it happens—not *if* it happens—it will excite the masses like nothing we have ever seen in sports. If you can remember the furor over Billie Jean King and Bobbie Riggs' tennis battle of the sexes . . . you can imagine how big this one will be."

Women have traditionally been hired to play baseball as a gate attraction, a way of drawing crowds and making money in hard times. The crowds came at first to see a novelty, but in order to keep the turnstiles clicking the woman had to be a *good* ballplayer. A packed stadium watched Jackie Mitchell and the Lookout Juniors take on Margaret Nabel and the New York Bloomer Girls because the fans expected to applaud, not laugh. They weren't disappointed.

That first ballplayer is out there now. She may be in T-ball or in Little League, or perhaps she has won a spot on a high school team somewhere. Organized baseball can find her . . . if it wants to. She can find organized baseball, too, but to enter it and succeed she needs the support and encouragement of fans everywhere. She also needs to know that behind her there are more young girls and women to come—players whose presence on the field and contribution to the game will truly make baseball our national pastime.

Photo and Permissions Acknowledgments

Courtesy of Don Allan: page 20; courtesy of Isabel Alvarez: pages 151, 152, 154, 155; AP/Wide World Photos: pages 77, 165, 193; *Atlanta Journal-Constitution:* page 181; courtesy of Bill Beverly: page 8; courtesy of *The Chattanooga News-Free Press:* page 67; *The Chicago Tribune:* page 194; courtesy of Helen Clement: page 18; courtesy of Julie Croteau: pages 200, 205; courtesy of Jean Faut Eastman: pages 142, 145, 148; courtesy of Rose Gacioch: pages 115, 116, 118; courtesy of Margaret Gisolo: pages 63, 64, 80; courtesy of Ray Hisrich: pages 1, 22, 24, 25, 26; courtesy of Edith Houghton: pages 37, 53, 55; courtesy of Sophie Kurys: page 124 (top); National Baseball Library, Cooperstown, New York: pages 10, 29, 45, 71, 94, 174, 186; from the collection of the Northern Indiana Historical Society: pages ii, 83 (all), 91, 93, 97, 105, 108, 111, 113, 122, 124 (bottom), 132, 135, 138, 146, 161; Mark Rucker, Transcendental Graphics: pages 14, 32, 33 (top), 34, 36, 46, 169; *The Sporting News:* page 191; courtesy of *The Tri-City Record:* pages 7, 33 (right); UPI/Bettmann: pages 75, 128; Urban Archives, Temple University, Philadelphia, Pennsylvania: page 58; courtesy of Joanne Winter: pages 98, 100; courtesy of Connie Wisniewski: page 101; courtesy of Lois Youngen: pages 158, 164.

Excerpt from the *Blue Book Supplement* on page 128 is reprinted with permission of the *Baseball Blue Book, Inc.;* *Sunday Herald Traveler* excerpt on page 189 is reprinted with permission of the *Boston Herald.*

Index

(Page numbers in italics refer to photographs only.)